AUSTRALIA
THE BEAUTIFUL

Managing Editor: Kerrie E. Andrews

Published by:
Kevin Weldon and Associates Pty Ltd
43 Victoria Street, McMahons Point N.S.W. 2060 Australia
Copyright Kevin Weldon and Associates Pty Ltd 1983

Typeset by: Walter Deblaere and Associates, Australia
Colour Separations: Rainbow Graphic Art, Hong Kong
Printed by: Mandarin Publishing, Hong Kong

National Library of Australia Cataloguing-in-Publication Data
Granville, James, 1942-
    Australia the beautiful.
    ISBN 0 949708 01 1.
    1. Australia — Description and travel — 1976-
    I. Beard, Colin. II. Title.
919.4'0463

Research: Anne Burke
Cover photograph: Leo Meier
Additional photography: Mark Hanlon and Peter Solness
Design, layout and assembly: Sue Williams and Lesley Workman
in association with Tony Gordon

AUSTRALIA
THE BEAUTIFUL

Text JAMES GRANVILLE
Photography COLIN BEARD

WATTLE
BOOKS

CONTENTS

OPPOSITE PAGE: *Autumnal landscapes help to endow Tasmania with the English atmosphere so often noted in towns such as Bothwell.*

PRECEDING TEN PAGES:
Pages 2/3: Kuranda Station in northern Queensland is on the rail link to the Atherton Tablelands.
Pages 4/5: A farmer droves his sheep over the 'long paddock' on a country road in Tasmania.
Pages 6/7: North of Broome in Western Australia is Lake Argyle, part of the Ord River Scheme and one of the largest man-made lakes in the world.
Pages 8/9: Fishermen compare notes after returning from their fishing grounds off the southern coast of New South Wales.
Pages 10/11: Grain silos on the horizon at sunset reflect the pastoral peace that belongs to the Avon Valley, near Perth in Western Australia.

FOREWORD

When we first conceived the idea for this book, we asked ourselves what ingredient was it that invoked a spirit of place more than any other in this country. Indeed, we asked ourselves whether the conventionally held view of a semi-arid inland region surrounded by a temperate coastline was any longer appropriate to describe Australia.

The answer to this question, of course, did not come so easily to us as we journeyed around the country. We still found ourselves observing Australia through the eyes of those who had gone before. Like those early pioneers, we found ourselves approaching the country as if it were, once more, a vast, inhospitable wasteland that had somehow to be crossed.

Our eyes, too, were somewhat blinded by a whole generation of Australian painters — men such as Sidney Nolan and Russell Drysdale. After all, they had left us with the legacy of their personally inspired symbols, all of which made it so much more difficult to establish our own.

Often, we were too eager to recognize their images in the country that we saw. Sun-bleached bones in the desert or a slab-bark hut silhouetted against the horizon, we later realized, reflect a fairly limited vision of the landscape. Luckily, however, we soon discovered that the truth of the matter lay in an altogether different direction.

In the process of travelling around the country, we began to look more closely at details within the landscape. Instead of seeking the monumental, we started to concentrate more on the minute. Ayers Rock may be one embodiment of Australia for many but for us it has already gone dangerously close to being divested of its awful presence through over-exposure. What had once been a sacred place of powerful significance to Aboriginals has now been reduced to an advertising logo for a building society.

More importantly, we began to form a new perception of what Australia is through its people. From our contact with widely differing groups in various parts of the continent, we were able to build up a picture of the country that was, thankfully, less reliant upon the almost mandatory picture of a cowboy outside the Birdsville Pub.

Australia the Beautiful, then, is a book about people, and how they relate to the land in which they have chosen to live. Whether we happened to be wandering down the main street of Broome on a hot afternoon or dipping our feet into the water off Seal Rocks, there was always someone nearby to make the experience seem more relevant.

For we might begin to talk about diving for pearls as in the first story *A Drink at the Roebuck.* Or we might learn something about lobster fishing from a fisherman at Seal Rocks, as described in *Lobster Layabout.*

At other times, we were able to gain new insight into the traditional nature of German culture in the hill towns of South Australia, as it is related in *All Things German.* These people, like their more English counterparts as described in *A Country Pilgrimage* through historic Tasmania, brought home to us the rich variety of cultures that exist even today within Australia.

Spider Murulu, the Aboriginal rock painter we met at Nourlangie in Kakadu National Park, was able to introduce us into his world in *Mimi Saga.* Through him we were able to understand — or at least begin to — the importance of the spirit-world to his people.

Looking for the Mahogany Ship provided us with the opportunity to explore a little known region of Victoria — the picturesque south-west — while in *It's Showtime* we shared in the excitement of Sydney's Royal Easter Show when the Grand Parade begins.

Pewter Plate Country allowed us a chance to investigate another historic area of Australia. Dutch shipwrecks and British settlers have inadvertently mingled around Geraldton, in Western Australia.

Last, in *Tropical Cocktail,* we were able to explore a lifestyle that is rapidly dying out in Australia. The world of a beachcomber on Queensland's tropical north coast still lingers on among the newly arrived alternative settlers who have come up from the south to replace the cane-cutters of old.

In each case, what made these places so attractive to us was embodied in the people that we met. Somehow, the way these people lovingly regarded their individual localities endowed the whole of Australia with a beauty that otherwise might have escaped us.

Detail makes *Australia the Beautiful* an intensely personal book. We sincerely hope that the reader will learn to enjoy a world of mimi figures, lobster pots, shipwrecks and lost caravels as much as we did.

OPPOSITE PAGE: Ruins of a mill house, constructed in the 19th century from locally hewn stone, at Greenough in Western Australia.

A Drink at the Roebuck

BROOME, WESTERN AUSTRALIA

Ever since our arrival in Western Australia
we had wanted to say that we had quenched our thirsts at the Roebuck Hotel
in Broome. But getting there turned out to be quite a pilgrimage.
Long straight roads lead nowhere, deserted stretches of coastline disappear
into nothing — these are the images that we have of our seemingly
endless journey up from the south.

Eventually, however, we made it. Driving down the main street
of Broome in the early morning was our first introduction to the cosmopolitan
life of this tropical township. Only three people were up and about.
Two Aboriginals were taking their morning stroll while Mr. Tack,
a Chinaman, was busy hauling down the shutters to his shop in
readiness for the brisk morning trade.

People, we found, don't get up early in Broome — there's no need.
A timeless air sustains the morning until around 9.00 a.m. when the Post
Office opens. Usually wearing worn thongs and short pants, people then
begin appearing on the main street. Shop doors are opened, the pearl shell
sorting sheds on the waterfront opposite the Roebuck rattle into life and
the locals begin to congregate on the verandah outside the hotel.

OPPOSITE PAGE: *Cable Beach, just outside Broome, is exemplary
of the majesty of Indian Ocean beaches. Cable Beach is the playground of
Broome's residents and visitors but the pearl-filled waters offshore
give Broome its more serious economic reason for existence.*
(Photo – Peter Solness)

'Jutting out from the foreshores of the town is a causeway,
obviously not the work of Nature, but considered by local historians
to have been built by Dampier's men to facilitate loading
and unloading when the Roebuck came into port. Tradition says
that, somewhere in the sand adjacent to the causeway, the
buccaneer buried treasure, but so far the secret of the covered-up
hoard, if there be any, has not been solved. '

(Sea, Land and Air, *November 1, 1921*)

Broome township and the ocean become an extension of each other around the jetty. On the long pier children watch while a pearl fisherman departs for his lugger moored in Roebuck Bay, beyond the tide's turn. Tides vary as much as six metres around Broome.

PRECEDING PAGE:
Ship ahoy! In Indian Ocean waters, when the sun sets over the horizon, luggers under sail and laden with pearl shells return from King Sound. (Photo – Peter Solness)

PEARLS have brought a lot of people to Broome over the years and the mystique still lures them today. Most of the divers working for the lugger captains around the turn of the century were either Japanese or Thursday Islanders. These men seemed to have the capacity to stay down longer than any other race; the ocean floor held no fears for them.

Still, they weren't the only races drawn to Broome during those heady days. Aboriginals, Malays, Koepangers, Singhalese, Malabar Men, Chinese and Tamils all flocked here to eke out an existence working for their European and Australian overlords. Nearly all the luggers were owned by Australians and companies like Streeter & Male employed most of the lugger captains. Broome has always been a company town.

Of course, there were occasional fights between the different racial communities. But these weren't as frequent as might be imagined. Most of the time people have lived alongside one another in relative harmony. The only racial disharmony that we saw during our stay was directed to the Aboriginals by the police. They still seem to delight in throwing these people in paddywaggons for trivial misdemeanours, even in the 1980s.

三田入萬靈

Peter Solness

Broome itself is a tapestry of people and places. The Japanese and Aboriginal and white Australians are just three of the resident races that give Broome a character unique to Australia. The graveyard in Broome is representative of the multi-racial nature of the people and is also a testimony to the many who died at sea, not only as a result of the dreaded bends but also because of the cyclones that seasonally ravage this stretch of coastline. In 1910, twenty-six luggers were lost along with the lives of forty men and, as late as 1935, one hundred and forty-one were drowned off the Lacepede Islands. Pearling has always been a risky business. For many years the Bon Matsuri festival, or Feast-of-the-Dead, was an annual event here amongst the Japanese community. It was celebrated to protect the souls of those who had died at sea.

Peter Solness

21

❝ Weird tales are current in Broome of pearls of wonderful lustre sold by night in lap-up time, and one of the most sordid took place in 1907. In that year a Jewish buyer named Leibgild was lured out one night by three Malays with the promise of a pearl for sale. He carried £300 in his clothes to make the purchase: was stabbed, robbed, and thrown into the creek. The Malays were quickly captured and hanged in Fremantle, and to add to the original story the decoy was not a pearl, but merely a glass marble from the neck of a lemonade bottle. ❞

(Sea, Land and Air, November 1, 1921)

The lugger memorial in the main park of Broome commemorates the deaths caused by the pearling industry. Life for the average diver was not easy. He made perhaps £20 a month, and for that he had to risk his life daily at depths of up to forty fathoms. If he was not harried by sharks or wandering manta rays, he was always subject to the risk of getting the agonising bends. The bends almost always meant certain death in the days before decompression chambers.

OPPOSITE PAGE AND RIGHT:
Pearl luggers berth at Broome Pier, but access to the pier can only be achieved at high tide, for the tides rise and fall up to six metres. Ever since the late 19th century, the town has been the pearling capital of Australia. At one time it was the pearling capital of the world and in 1908 there were over 370 luggers based in Broome. In that year alone, some 2500 people worked directly in the industry. Between them they hauled up from the deep over £190,000 worth of pearl shell and nearly £75,000 worth of pearl. Lugger hulks on the sand among the mangroves and on the beach are mute testimony to the heyday of pearling in Broome.

Famed entrance to the Roebuck Bay Hotel in Broome. The Roebuck should be immortalised on a postcard, not because of any inherent picturesque qualities — far from it — but because of its character. No other hotel in Australia is quite so rakishly obtrusive, nor so little endowed with any architectural presence of its own. And yet it is a place that you would never wish to pass by, even if you were a teetotaller. The Roebuck Bay Hotel embodies the essential spirit of the north-west of this country in the way that the Harbour Bridge sums up Sydney.

All nationalities congregate at the Roebuck in the morning, afternoon and evening to drink and share in the conversation.

PRECEDING PAGE:
The lugger Buccleuch in the process of being outfitted for its next voyage out to the pearl grounds. The buoys, carrying the lugger's identification, register the Buccleuch's diving areas when at sea.

William Dampier, the first European navigator to record his visit to the shores around Broome in the late 17th century, named Roebuck Bay after his ship. He also pronounced it 'the most barren spot on the face of the earth'. Apart from recording his impressions of kangaroos ('they look like racoons'), he did little to encourage future settlement.

Still, William Dampier's voyage has left an indelible mark on the world. His journals were later published in England, inspiring the great satirist of his age, Jonathon Swift, to pen *Gulliver's Travels*. Swift located Lillyput somewhere off the coast of Broome. Broome became a name in the history books for other events as well. In 1942 Imperial Japanese dive-bombers attacked the town from the air. They sank numerous luggers and destroyed a number of Dornier aircraft moored in the Bay. Many Dutch refugees lost their lives that day.

For myself and Colin, sitting in the bar of the Roebuck Hotel later that morning, the history of the place only served to heighten the sense of the exotic that we perceived in Broome. That town lives in the past yet tries to put on a brave front for the present and it's all epitomised in the Roebuck.

We went to Broome to rub shoulders with the world at the Roebuck Bay Hotel. I have drunk with the best of them at some of the most memorable bars in the world. Places such as Quinn's Bar in Tahiti in its heyday and Dimitri's on the other side of the Atlas Mountains in Morocco still raise pleasant memories. The Roebuck, though, will always remain a more vivid experience because there I re-discovered the rakish charm that so epitomised Australian outback towns in the past.

'Sure, we get drunk occasionally,' one of the locals remarks. 'But that's our way of letting off steam.'
'Once it's over, though, we climb in our plane and fly back to the property,' his mate adds.
'Yeah. You'll never see hide nor hair of us until the next time.' The first man grins at the evident absurdity of his own remark.
'We work like navvies and we drink like fish. That's the way we like it,' his mate affirms.

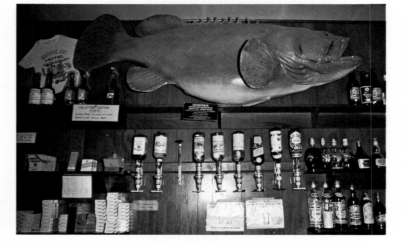

The one that did not get away is enshrined above the bar at the Roebuck. Locals often pass their spare time fishing, both in the estuaries and out in the deeper waters of the Indian Ocean where groper is a covetted prize.

The main street of Broome is dominated by corrugated iron, raised footpaths and shops owned by people with names that indicate their Asian origin. Chinese shopkeepers supply the town with the essentials of life as well as a few of the luxuries. Mr Tack, who knows his business, offers everything from radios to confectionary. His father was the best pearl doctor in town.

Tropical architecture is as typical in north-western Western Australia as it is in Queensland. Raised floors allow air to circulate and cool beneath the house while shaded verandahs provide a cooling effect for air passing through the house itself.

Across the road in one of the pearlshell sorting sheds, men are still sitting on old boxes with handkerchiefs over their noses while they sort through the shell, much as they did a hundred years ago. Nothing really changes in Broome because people living there believe the town is Shangri-la anyway.

Mr. Tack, who lives on the main street, has a quiet and conscribed life. As a small merchant, he sells anything from spices to Solvol soap. He usually sits outside his shop on a wooden box and observes the world as it passes by with unblinking eyes. Probably he has his memories; his father before him was known as the best pearl doctor in town.

The pearl doctor used to be, and still is, one of the most important links in the economic chain of pearling. For it is he who must peel back the layers of imperfect nacre on the surface of a pearl. Using such instruments as an obsidian knife or a small file stuck in a champagne cork, his job is to work on the pearl to the point where he believes the gem has reached its most perfect state. Peeling beyond this point might ruin the pearl; or it might reveal a more limpid beauty. That is the risk he has to take.

The ultimate pearl quality in the old days was known as 'la desirée'. But the stages before this had equally fascinating titles, such as 'silver-clouded moon', 'gleaming-crystal', 'pool-at-dawn' and 'starlight-on-a-frosty-night' — qualities to be reckoned with in the world of Mr. Tack's father and grandfather.

Just up the road from Mr. Tack's shop is Mr. Tang's café where you can eat some of the best Chinese food this side of Singapore while Mr. Tang's father peels onions out the back. In fact, wherever you go in Broome, you encounter the faded tapestry of the past. A large, corrugated building known as the Sun Picture Theatre further up the road could probably put on a silent movie without raising an eyebrow around town.

Each year, the locals stage the Festival of the Pearl in the town park. Entertainers, jugglers, satay booths, game tents, fairy floss stands and junk gift shops blossom like hibiscus on the grass. Everyone comes to town to join in the fun. Broad-brimmed stetsons merge with flower-patterned saris as men and women from diverse cultures wander amongst the booths. Even the modern day Japanese come away from their pearl farms, further down the Bay, to share in the annual festivities and the flowing beer.

Tang's Café, cuisine capital of the north-west, is famous for its chop suey. It is surrounded by red, yellow and
blue neon lights and, once inside, there is a sense of eating in a gold-fish bowl.
At the back of the café, Mr. Tang's old, partly blind father sits in one corner peeling onions by instinct.
Perhaps he too remembers the days when the pearl reigned supreme in Broome.

Then there's the famous Sun Picture Theatre.
Behind the facade is an open-air hall filled with
deck chairs. Taped piano music presenting
Winifred Atwell at the keyboard welcomes
you as you file past two projectionists standing
in a cubicle above the main entrance.
Even Laurel and Hardy might have chuckled
at this theatrical environment.

Cable Beach, one of the many fine beaches around Broome, makes the area an idyllic tourist playground. Windsurfing and the transition of colours between midday and sunset caused us to visit Cable Beach on more than one occasion.

While Broome happens to be a part of the Australian mainland, it nevertheless lives a life of its own. If the locals had their way, they would probably print their own stamps! Of course, the tourists flock to the place in season and pretend they're living in another world. The Sun Picture Theatre might condescend to put on a film in living Technicolor for the benefit of visitors such as ourselves, but these intrusions have little effect on the town. The locals continue to scuff their thongs on the verandah of the Roebuck Bay Hotel at nine o'clock each morning as they wait for the bar doors to open. Corrugated iron roofs still bake in the hot north-western sun and the faces of a dozen races will remain dedicated to Broome's lifestyle.

Mimi Saga

SACRED CAVES OF THE TOP END

In the shadow of one of Australia's richest uranium deposits
at Jabiru in the Northern Territory lies an equally rich conglomerate of myths
and legends handed down to us from the time of Dreaming. On the very edge
of Arnhem Land, not far from the junction of South Alligator River
and Nourlangie Creek, caves filled with rock art frescoes and drawings
preserve for all time the sacred mythical life of the Australian Aboriginals.

I had always wanted to visit the Nourlangie caves ever since
my first encounter with pre-historic rock art in the Central Sahara. There,
I had witnessed the beginnings of human expression — in fact,
the very beginnings of culture as we know it.

The similarity does not end there. What the pre-historic tribal
people of the Hoggar Mountains in the Central Sahara pictured in their
painting varies only in style to what our own Aboriginals sought to depict.
At the Top End I had once more made that journey back in time to
the very origins of Man.

*OPPOSITE PAGE: Sacred male figure painted in the 'X-ray' style at
Nourlangie Rock, Kakadu National Park. Executed in ochres, pipeclay,
charcoal and sometimes blood, these paintings are often found in
inaccessible places which can only be reached by notched pole
or native ladder.*

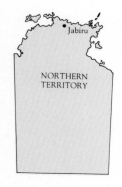

The Nourlangie escarpment broods over the surrounding country; a sense of the omnipotence of nature is inescapable in this region.

Spider Murulu, one of Australia's least known artists, learnt his craft from his father after years of apprenticeship. Today, he renews the sacred Dreaming figures of his family clan by painting over the faded ochres. Spider's inspiration comes from tradition, not from himself; unlike modern artists, he relies on a time-honoured message that has been handed down to him.

TODAY, the once arduous journey out to the South Alligator from Darwin is made much easier since the Arnhem Highway has been sealed. Our Land Cruiser made excellent time along the unbending stretch of tar; we passed through clumps of tropical scrubland as we neared what is now known as Kakadu National Park. We were anxious, however, to make contact with our guide, Spider Murulu, a member of a local Aboriginal group.

Spider is an old man now but ever since his youth he has been familiar with the art of painting on cave walls. Like his forefathers, Spider is conscious that his talent for evoking images from the Dreaming must be carefully honed if his people are to survive.

Even though he is a Christian, Spider still holds to the old beliefs. I recall one day how, when we were sitting cross-legged by the fire, a tiny whirlwind suddenly began to approach our camp, raising a red film of dust from the ground.

Spider immediately rose to his feet and tossed a handful of sand into the wind. Then he sang: 'Ngalorgarangalorgarang'. Smiling, he turned to me and explained. 'That's the way the old people told Ngalorgara (the Whirlwind) which way to go.'

PRECEDING SIX PAGES:
Pages 34-35: Moon rising over an escarpment in Kakadu National Park.
Pages 36-39: Overlooking one of the numerous swamp plains that appear during the wet season in the area.
OPPOSITE PAGE: *Northern blue-winged kookaburra.*

No-one knows for certain the true age of the cave paintings that are in the care of men such as Spider. Though many of the motifs deal with the mythological figures and their exploits, others reflect the Aboriginals' early contact with alien visitors. Not only are the Macassan islanders to the north of Australia represented but also Europeans holding early muskets and flintlocks.

The cave paintings, presumably, reach much further back into antiquity. They depict both the mythical life of the Aboriginals as well as normal daily activities. Whether they are depicting kangaroo, echidna or crocodile, the paintings testify to an apparent abundance of game before the coming of white man.

Fish, too, swim across the ochred surface of these walls. Elsewhere, these great rock galleries — in many respects Australia's answer to the Altamira of Spain and Les Eyzies of France — are the last sacred hunting grounds of the magical Mimi people.

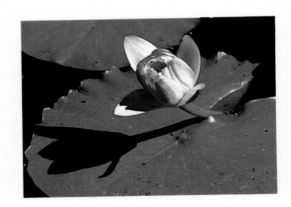

After the monsoonal rains, the land is transformed into a vast swamp. A natural haven for waterbirds, these swamps are part of the complex ecosystem of northern Australia. Without the proper rituals being performed by Spider and his people, the cyclical rains might not eventuate.

When we arrived at South Alligator Creek, Spider was waiting for us. He was anxious to take us out to Nourlangie Creek as soon as possible. It was as though he very much wanted to be close to his beloved Mimi people.

'Come on,' he muttered, climbing into the back of our Land Cruiser. 'We betta be gittin' out there pretty soon.'

'But we've only just arrived,' I said.

'Doan matter. If you fellas wanna see some cave pichers, you betta git a move on.'

So we reluctantly left the South Alligator Inn and journeyed along a rough dirt track towards Nourlangie. Recent rains had turned the region into a flood plain and it was difficult in places to negotiate the mired road.

Still, we finally recognised Nourlangie Rock rising like a monolith at the far end of a shallow valley. Here we were for the first time, gazing at an ancient rock outcrop that had been the traditional art gallery for Spider's people since the beginning of time. One thing was certain: Spider's ancestors had a fine understanding of landscape. They had chosen this place for their spirit centre with the same acute sense of place as the ancient Greeks did their sanctuaries.

'This a pretty good place,' Spider remarked, the tone of his voice almost reverent. 'My father, he come up here to put paint on our family pichers even when I was a kid.'

'And that's what you continue to do today, Spider,' I said.

'Someone's gotta do it. Otherwise they be dyin' pretty quick.'

'Who would die?'

'The Spirits,' Spider added, pursing his lips. 'Lightning Man and all the others gotta be looked after, yer know.'

'What about the Rainbow Snake?' I asked.

'Sure, him too. He pretty important. If he not kept in good order things'll go bad pretty soon.'

Thus Spider introduced us to the various classifications of Spirit figures up there in his beloved caves. Like a museum curator, he was able to explain how he and his friends took care of their respective family sacred sites. For these cave paintings of the Top End are more than museum pieces; they are the one vital link that Spider and his people have with the past.

*Natural patterns in the landscape of
Kakadu . . . waterlilies thrive in the swamplands of
the Northern Territory, particularly after
the monsoon.*

*Home to a most important part of Australia's art heritage, the Nourlangie escarpment
is a sandstone rock massif on the western Arnhem Land plateau.*

Delicate arabesque formed by vegetation in the fading light of dusk.

Finally, we left the Land Cruiser and approached Nour-langie Rock on foot. Here we were, making our way along a narrow path back into the Dreaming, with only Spider to act as guide if ever we became lost.

Once we had climbed under the ledge of rock we found ourselves in another world. Above us, the cave walls were a virtual pantheon of sacred figures, animals, fish and myste-rious mythological detail. The Aboriginal Dreaming has a unique flavour of its own: of random battles between men and gods, of a time when the Spirit figures crept out from their haven under earth.

'Pretty nice pichers, eh?' Spider spoke with evident pride.

I nodded. 'Who are those stick-like figures, Spider?' I asked.

'Them's Mimi people. Hunters and warriors. It's them that fought the big battles to protect our tribe.'

'How do you keep in contact with all these Spirit people?'

'Oh, I come up here and put new paint on 'em,' Spider answered. 'That way they comin' alive again 'n' talk to me when I'm not feelin' good.'

Here we had the simplicity of a very ancient ritual explained to us. Spider's method of making contact with his ancestors is not unlike the renewal process that goes on each Sunday in church. Eating the sacramental bread finds its parallel in Spider's actions of putting new paint on his figures.

OPPOSITE PAGE: *A hunter of the Mimi spirit-hero genre, complete
with game bag and spears. Mimi figures are one-dimensional and
usually painted in one colour only, representing an earlier art form
than that of the 'X-ray' type.*

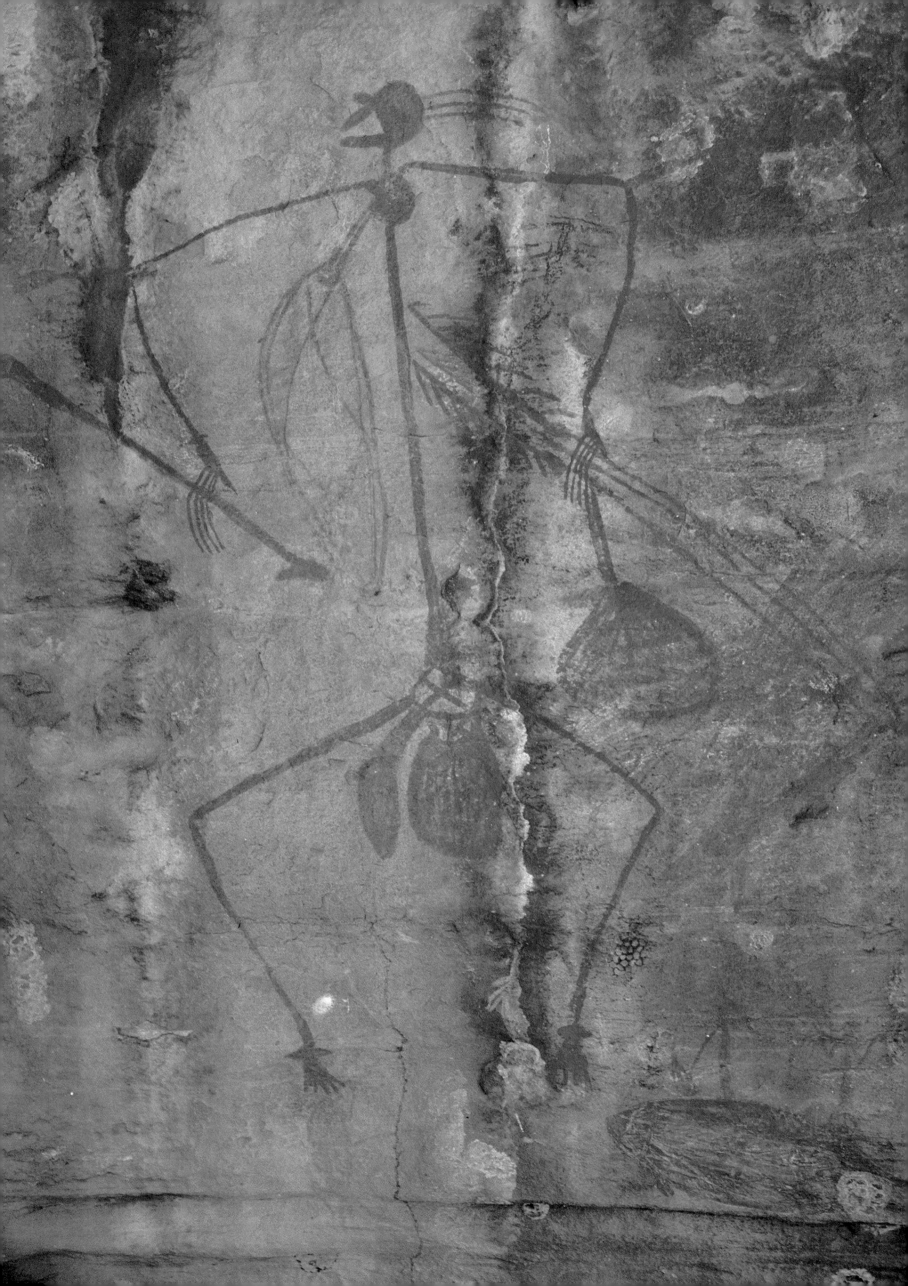

❛ *The most interesting things, and what we came up to see, were the rock shelters of natives, where they rest in the cool of the evening during fine weather, or are protected from the monsoonal rains during the wet season, when the flats below are transformed into swamps. The slanting roofs and sides were one mass of native drawings, precisely similar to those done on bark, but here, the rocks had been blackened for long years by the smoke of countless camp fires and the drawings, most of them fishes, had been superimposed on one another, the brighter colours of the more recent ones standing out clearly on the darker background. Here and there were groups of stencilled hands and feet. On other rock shelters on the hills along the Alligator River, the drawings were not superimposed and comprised fishes, turtles, crocodiles and snakes.* ❜*

(from Spencer, Sir Baldwin,* Wanderings in Wild Australia, *Volume II, Macmillan, London, 1928.)*

Obiri Rock silhouetted like a ponderous human head. Around the base of this massive sandstone outcrop are caves filled with rock paintings that date back centuries.

We soon understood more about the various styles that occur in Aboriginal rock art when we journeyed north from South Alligator Creek to Obiri Rock. Another distinctive rock outcrop on a plain, Obiri is the home of some fine examples of 'X-ray' art.

Finely rendered barramundi often overlay much older paintings that have subsequently lost their significance to later generations of Aboriginals. Nevertheless, the unusual nature of the 'X-ray' style makes it possible to recognise every aspect of the fish or animal's cosmic life.

Not only is its skeleton rendered exactly but also its internal organs. Since the Aboriginals are keen observers of nature, they are thus able to enter completely the spirit of their painting. It is this total empathy with their subject which makes it possible for Spider and his friends to paint such delicate masterpieces of traditional art.

Coming away from Obiri Rock, I was left with the same sense of exhilaration that I have felt on occasion when walking out of the Louvre Museum in Paris or the National Gallery in London.

Art, essentially, is a celebration — not only of the living process as seen through the complex eye of Man but also of his relationship with the metaphysical world.

At Nourlangie and Obiri Rocks we had witnessed this celebration. And at the same time, we had encountered one of Australia's great unknown artists: Spider Muluru of the Ngalgbon tribe.

PRECEDING PAGE: *A fine example of the 'X-ray' style presents a traditional dance sequence celebrated by women.*

OPPOSITE PAGE: *Aboriginal art depicts all the interests and preoccupations relevant to the continuation of tribal life. At Kakadu, often-repeated motifs dealing with fish, the kangaroo and crocodile, Namorado Spirits and Lightning-men all combine to give us a vivid picture of life in Australia before the arrival of European man.*

' I could not help reflecting, as I examined with interest the various objects represented — the human figures, the animals, the birds, the weapons, the domestic implements, the scenes of savage life — on the curious frame of mind that could induce these uncultivated people to repair, perhaps at stated seasons of the year, to this lonely picture gallery, to admire and add to the productions of their forefathers. No doubt they expended on their works of art as much patience and labour and enthusiasm as ever was exhibited by a Raphael or a Michelangelo in adorning the walls of St. Peter or the Vatican; and perhaps the admiration and applause of their fellow-countrymen imparted as much pleasure to their minds as the patronage of popes and princes, and the laudation of the civilized world to the great masters of Italy. '

(from Stokes, J. L., Discovery in Australia with an account of the coast and rivers explored and surveyed during the voyage of the H.M.S. Beagle in the years 1837-1843, Volume II, Boone, London, 1846.)

Turtles and fish are often repeated in the art of the region, indicating their importance to the people. The barramundi is also rendered with particularly fine technique and here overlooks a male and female figure.

OPPOSITE PAGE AND PRECEDING PAGE:
Obiri Rock lends Kakadu panoramic grandeur, but the valley, when viewed from under one of Obiri's massive ledges, emphasises the Rock's majestic and mysterious qualities long recognised by the Aboriginal people.

Obiri Rock invokes its own solemn sense of architecture, even at dusk.

An egret at rest after eating in the swampland below.

Nature indulges in its own art form typical in the region. Form, texture, light and shade are magnificently displayed in the ancient, weathered mushroom boulders of Spider's country.

Lobster Layabout

SEAL ROCKS, NEW SOUTH WALES

I have always wanted to discover somewhere in Australia a small fishing community that lives off the bounty of the sea in a way that men did before sophisticated sonar equipment and nets came along to change their lives.

Many fishing fleets dot the Australian coastline but none are quite like the one at Seal Rocks, New South Wales. Here I found the setting for which I had been searching, for here men and their families live by the sea in a manner that has changed little since this stretch of coastline was first inhabited.

A steep, rain-rutted track must be negotiated in order to reach the beach but, once this is done, one is confronted with much more than a mere panorama of white sand. Above the tide line and overlooked by a tiny Moorish-style lighthouse on the headland, a row of fishing boats rests on the sand like Agamemnon's fleet.

Unlike their ocean-going counterparts, these white-painted, clinker-built boats have no cabins. The decks are quite flat in order to store lobster pots and the only features are a diesel engine and a large hold for storing lobsters and fish.

OPPOSITE PAGE: Below Sugarloaf Point lighthouse, the Pacific Ocean surges along a natural rock canyon when there is a storm at sea, creating a natural blowhole.

NEW SOUTH WALES

Seal Rocks

Sugarloaf Point lighthouse and outbuildings on the headland above Seal Rocks. Since the Rainbow foundered here in 1864, the lighthouse has served coastal shipping well. The seals that live on the rocks were remarked upon by the early explorers and continue to attract visitors to the area.

THE tradition of trapping lobsters in the waters off Seal Rocks goes back to the time when a Greek fisherman first settled on this beach at the turn of the century. It was he, so locals like Alex Campbell will tell you, who brought with him the technique of building lobster pots and laying them in patterns out at sea.

Not only did the Greek make an adequate living out of lobster potting — he used to sell his catch to the passing coastal steamers — but in time he also managed to build a white-stuccoed hermitage on the hillside above the beach. Perhaps he dreamed of his island home back in Greece.

Today nothing remains of that old Greek's cottage, only the memory of his endeavour. However, Alex Campbell and his fellow fishermen still build their traps in the way that he taught their fathers.

Each morning on the tide the ritual begins. Alex and his mates wander sleepy-eyed down the hillside from their cottages and gather on the beach. Someone starts the tractor and positions it at the bow of one of the fishing boats. While the others guide the boat, the tractor slowly pushes the boat down the beach into the water.

PRECEDING SIX PAGES:
Pages 62-67: The bay at Seal Rocks is a natural harbour protected from the southerlies by a reef of rocks. The fishermen are able to haul their boats out of the sea without having to contend with pounding waves. Come morning, they push their boats into the water with the aid of a tractor and, after the day's fishing, the boats are hauled from the sea by a machine-driven pulley housed near the chilling shed above the beach.

The fishing fleet is pulled up onto the beach not far from the local fishermen's cottages. To the south, the rocks that give the beach its name belie the turbulent waters and jagged outcrops of the reef.

❛ *The Seal Rocks were discovered (but not named) by Lieutenant Flinders in July 1799,*
when exploring the coast of Sydney in the sloop Norfolk, 25 tons, in search of a large river which
might carry him into the interior. "We sailed out of Port Jackson on July 8, and next morning
came in with a part of the coast, north of Port Stephens, which Captain Cook passed in the night.
Off a projection which I called Sugarloaf Point in latitude 32 degrees, 29 min, lie two rocks to
the south-eastward, at the distance of two and four miles. We passed between these rocks and the
point, and kept close in with the shore as far to the north as the hills called Three Brothers."
No point on the coast is better guarded. The lighthouse stands 258 ft above the sea.
Nearly a century has passed since the rocks were made known, without any recorded calamity having
occurred there and now, when navigation has reached its highest point of perfection, and
the seaman has every kind of assistance that science can give him, one of the most terrible wrecks that
has happened on our coasts has taken place at that very spot. ❜

(from The Evening News, *August 17, 1895 page 3*)

With the aid of tractor and rollers, the boats are pushed over one set of rollers and another set is placed on the sand at the stern to receive the keel. Alex Campbell is one of the oldest inhabitants of Seal Rocks and has spent all his life trapping lobsters and catching fish. Like the other men, he washes down his catch during the return trip home and at the end of the day he runs his boat up onto the sand in preparation for a tow up the beach.

Loaded up with fresh bait and a few replacement lobster pots, each fisherman chugs off to his respective lobster ground to check his traps. On a calm day they may even find themselves accompanied by the local herd of seals. The seals launch themselves off the rocks of the headland and have given Seal Rocks its name.

Overhead, starlings and seagulls wheel in the morning air. They, too, anticipate the prospect of a fair catch. However, because it is so late in the season, Alex Campbell is not so confident.

'The crawling season's almost over,' he admitted to me as his boat dipped and rose in the swell. 'Lobsters stop crawling in the winter months and once that happens we have to rely on what fish we can catch.'

'What do you do in the winter, then?' I asked.

'There's plenty to keep you occupied. We have to haul up the traps and bring 'em back to the beach to dry out. Usually half of them've rotted away.'

'Which means you have to build some more?'

'Yeah,' replied Alex, adjusting his salt-bleached hat over his face. 'We have to go out back in the bush and cut down some turpentine wood. We use this sort of wood because it resists cobra — that's a type of sea borer. A well made trap will last up to four years.'

'How do you catch your bait?' I asked.

'We catch 'em when the fish are biting along the beach. That's usually in spring when they've been washed down the rivers after the rain.'

'You net them, I suppose.'

Alex Campbell grinned. His deeply tanned face lined as he recalled how they all work together to net the beach fish.

'Everyone helps, including mum and the kids. It's a big day, catching them mullet, bream and blackfish. In the old days we used to hang 'em up on long trestles at the far end of the beach to dry out. Nowadays we do it back in the bush.' Alex nodded his head contemptuously towards the beach. 'Tourists that come down in the weekends started to complain about the smell.'

The trestles of drying fish are now concealed in the bush; the one I stumbled upon was in a small clearing. Aside from the sharp stench of dead fish, dipped in brine and browning like toast in the sun, I noticed a dead seagull hanging on a piece of cord attached to a pole. 'That's to frighten away the other birds,' Alex told me when I enquired the purpose.

The fishing community of Seal Rocks has withstood the ravages of storms and time. The fishermen's cottages seem rooted to the hillside and Mrs Campbell is an integral part of the place. A quiet chat with a friend reflects the sense of community one experiences in Seal Rocks.

PRECEDING PAGE:
Seagulls flock to the returning boats as the fish are gutted. Calm water and tasty morsels thrown from Alex's boat make Seal Rocks a seagull's haven.

In all the years that men have been potting lobsters off Seal Rocks, not one serious accident has occurred, perhaps because of the Sugarloaf Point lighthouse which is always there to guide them homewards after dusk. The lighthouse was built in 1875 and has a white flash of one million candle-power. It can be seen from as far away as forty-eight kilometres and is one of the few left in Australia that is still manned by a lighthouse keeper.

'They built it after the *Rainbow* went down off the beach in 1864,' Alex told me. 'They lost seven lives that night during the storm. The rest of the crew and the passengers had to walk 110 kilometres into Port Stephens.'

'Is that part of the old ship you can see at low tide on the beach?' I asked.

Alex Campbell nodded. 'That's her boiler, all right.'

So little had changed around here, I realised. The fishermen still build their boats in the same way as they did before WW I and still they name them after their girlfriends or wives. They still construct traps the way they were taught by their fathers. And still they teach their sons how to steer a heavily laden fishing boat through the waves towards the beach. Most of all, they are still careful to point out the half-submerged reef that was once the *Rainbow*'s boiler.

'I can remember the days when we couldn't get in so easily to Bungwahl to do our shopping,' Alex told me. 'So we used to eat fish, shoot a wallaby for meat and collect seabirds' eggs for breakfast. Them days've gone now, though,' he added, smiling wistfully as he remembered. Even the great schools of whales that used to swim up the coast to the warmer northern waters have disappeared.

'We . . . agreed to try whether sealing would not answer and accordingly we went
200 miles to the Northward to a seal rock between Port Stephens and Port Macquarie . . . We had
two or three narrow escapes from being capsized in surfs whilst attempting to land on
the seal island . . . we were attempting to get through a surf to go to some rocks, when the boat
broached-to and capsized and all hands were thrown out of her. I don't know how I got safe
to the beach, but I found that I had narrowly escaped being knocked senseless by a blow of the steer
oar which barely cleared my head as the boat was pitched by the violence of the surf . . . The next
day I walked, or rather limped along, with a party of natives, to a beach 30 miles distant; being
bare footed I felt considerable difficulty in keeping up with my dark companions, and the sand
made my sores still worse. When we reached our journey's end we found a few natives broiling
snapper fish on the embers of a fire. They had caught a large quantity that day and we all partook of
this fare with keen appetites, and at night lay down, native-like by the side of a fire and slept, men,
women and children indiscriminately, one amongst another. I was tired out and
did not awake once throughout the night.'

(from the papers of John Boultbee, written at an unknown date between 1834 and his death in 1854.)

A region of often stark contrasts,
Seal Rocks and its environs nevertheless
possess a natural beauty of their own.

Though the fish still bite along the beach every spring and Alex Campbell and his mates still tend their pots, one wonders how long the fragile harmony of their lives at Seal Rocks will last. The long fingers of tourism are already reaching their secluded haven. A camping ground exists where once their bait hung out in the sun to dry. Even the old woman in her shop on the hill stocks comics and tee-shirts for the kids.

'The main thing,' I said to Alex Campbell, 'is to stick to doing what you do best and not to give in.'

He only shrugged. 'I don't know whether we'll pull any lobsters today. Still, we might get a fish or two for dinner,' he added.

I watched as the distant coastline disappeared for a moment behind a wall of water. At the same time, I wished in my heart that the old Greek might return to keep company with Alex Campbell and his friends once more.

In the back country behind Seal Rocks the bush has provided a hideaway for the drying of bait.
Once the process took place on the beach until the tourists began objecting; now the fishermen build trestles over which
the fish are draped far from the visitors' noses. Between two and three weeks must elapse before
the raw fish are adequately cured and ready for storing.

Further out in the back country is Myall Lake, a haven for naturalists and fishermen alike.

PRECEDING PAGES:
Pages 82/83: The beauty of Myall Lakes National Park attracts holidaymakers
who fish the waters and spend lazy days cruising the waterways.
Pages 84/85: The tranquil setting of Tahlee was chosen for the site of
the Australian Agricultural Company. It was at Tahlee in 1829 that Sir William
Parry, the celebrated Arctic explorer, arrived with his wife Isabella to take up
the position of Commissioner for the Australian Agricultural Company.

The nearby oyster beds at Tahlee on
Port Stephens offer a different kind of bounty
from the sea. Once the important outpost from
which the Australian Agricultural Company
spread northward along the Karuah Valley
in 1825, the town has since disappeared.

Oyster picker breaking up oyster shells in the bottom of his barge.

The convict-built stone church at Tahlee is now a youth hostel. The first stone was laid by Captain Phillip King R. N. on 17 December, 1846. The church also has a ship's bell from the schooner Carrington, lost at sea in 1842.

Whether Seal Rocks and its environs remain an unspoilt natural setting is in the hands of all those living in the area. Unchecked development and too many tourist facilities may force the fishermen to quit their beloved beach and fishing grounds. If such an event were to happen, the charm of Seal Rocks would be lost to us forever.

Uniting Church in Australia
· Chalmers Church ·
1848

A Country Pilgrimage

HISTORICAL TOWNS IN TASMANIA

Very few States in Australia are more richly endowed with so much that is of historical interest than Tasmania. One of the country's earliest settled colonies, Tasmania has taken great trouble in recent times to preserve its vast heritage, both for Tasmanians and visitors alike.

To journey along the inland route from Launceston in the north to Hobart and points south is to make a pilgrimage of an unusual kind. Unlike the great pilgrimage routes to places like Canterbury or Rome in Medieval Europe, there may not be an ancient monastery or Gothic cathedral in which to rest one's tired feet; but what lies concealed behind the green and rambling hills of this island State provides a glimpse of another, more homely sort of grandeur.

Indeed, the journey south from Launceston unveils a plethora of historical townships, country estates and architectural styles to satisfy any wanderer. Even in Launceston itself, a township founded by Col. William Paterson in 1805, there is a quaint village air of parkland and church steeples.

A few kilometres further south and we were at once introduced into the world of stately homes that was so popular among early colonists intent on evoking images of the Old Country amongst their new surroundings.

OPPOSITE PAGE: *The spire of Chalmers Uniting Church, Launceston, in the Neo-Gothic Revival style, pierces the almost tangible blue of the Tasmanian sky.*

91

Glass house in the grounds of Entally House.

O NE of the oldest establishments is Entally House, built by Thomas Reibey II in 1819, after his arrival in the Colony. He managed to surround himself with all the accoutrements considered necessary for a 19th century gentleman to survive in the Colonies.

Thus this house was equipped with a chapel of its own, a music room, a reading room and stables in addition to the normal living quarters. He also lovingly endowed his property with neatly arranged English-style gardens and a green house. Today, Entally House is a carefully preserved museum filled with antiques of the period.

Evandale is a classified historical town. Named in 1836 in honour of Tasmania's first Surveyor-General, G. W. Evans, the township is closely associated with two well known painters of Australian landscapes — John Glover and Tom Roberts. Both these men are buried in the district. Originally settled by Norfolk Islanders in 1816, Evandale exudes a stately Georgian air of towering statues and classical facades.

Towns like Ross, a few kilometres down the road, stand as a constant reminder of the energy and foresight of one of Australia's early colonial Governors, Lachlan Macquarie. He established a military outpost here in 1812 and within a few years it was a thriving agricultural settlement.

John Lee Archer, the Government Architect of the day, recommended that a freestone bridge of 'beauty and durability' be built over the river named after Macquarie. Today, this bridge still spans the river — an elegant legacy left to us from the days when much of the stonework was carried out by convicts.

PRECEDING SIX PAGES:
Pages 92/95: Bothwell developed as a centre for agricultural settlement and as a military outpost. Early settlers built their homesteads and estates in the Georgian style. The land, too, was portioned off in much the same way as was traditional in England. Wentworth House is a two-storey construction built in 1833 with an asymmetrical portico and windows and doors flanked by pilasters.
Page 96/97: Ross Bridge was designed by John Lee Archer and opened by Governor Arthur in 1836. The convict Daniel Herbert was given a free pardon for his stone carvings that employed Celtic symbols and motifs of animal and human heads.

Bluestone chapel under a shingle roof, Entally House.

Entally House at Hadspen is a single-storey vernacular house which has been altered many times during its life. Of painted brick, it has a shingled hipped roof, a single-storey veranda and a four-panel front door; verdant lawns grace the courtyard. The interior of Entally House reflects the casual elegance of the period.

The coach house and stables of Entally House. Now operating as an historic museum, Entally House is open to visitors.

Entally House shelters some fascinating 19th century equipment, including a steam driven tractor, farm machinery still in running order and a penny farthing bicycle.

A pastoral town since 1816, Evandale was settled by Norfolk Islanders. The town is set in a landscape of hedgerows, windbreaks and copses and was named in honour of Tasmania's first Surveyor-General, G. W. Evans. John Batman, the founder of Melbourne, lived here for fifteen years prior to embarking for his farming venture at Port Phillip Bay, Victoria.

❝ *We give a View of Clarendon, the seat of the late James Cox, Esq., one of the oldest of the Tasmanian colonists, and a gentleman held in the highest esteem among all classes of the community . . . The park is of great extent, and abounds with kangaroo, emus, and deer. The first stag hunted in Tasmania was from the Clarendon park, and the liberal proprietor (who was a lover of every manly sport) often furnished one for a similar purpose.* ❞

('Clarendon, Evandale, Tasmania', The Illustrated Melbourne Post, May, 1866)

The old churches and hotels such as the Clarendon Arms highlight the different architectural styles of region. Antiques shop such as Village Antiques are a common feature on the road south to Hobart.

Oatlands was also a military outpost that made the successful transition to a provincial agricultural centre. Set on the shores of Lake Dulverton, the town boasts consistent and continuous streetscapes highlighted by the original old mill. Most of the early buildings in the township are constructed from locally hewn sandstone.

So our pilgrimage along the route to Hobart continued as neatly ordered towns containing rustic old pubs on street corners greeted our gaze. As well, we always found a public garden, filled with flowers or a row of elms, to soften the eye. Tasmania is a landscape of subtle nuances as well as being famous for its wilderness areas. The old ways of arranging the environment are still held dear amongst its inhabitants. People in this region are a gentle bunch, perhaps reflecting the peaceful nature of their environment: little has changed over the last hundred years and perhaps they don't really want it to.

The town of Bothwell, for example, resides in an extensively modified landscape. Traces of the original countryside are almost lost among English-style fields, Georgian estates and stands of gold-leafed poplars. Originally known as Upper Clyde, the predominantly Scottish settlers of the region petitioned Governor Arthur to rename their town Bothwell.

The names of two towns further south from here have an interesting history. Jericho and Bagdad were both named by the early explorer, Hugh Germaine. It was said that his only reading while on expedition was *The Bible* and *The Arabian Nights*. So he named the regions that he discovered with exotic sounding names drawn from these two books.

Kempton is well known for its gymkhana held each February. Named after Anthony Fenn Kemp, who was given a grant of land here, Kempton is graced with a magnificently preserved old church dating back to 1841. The Wilmot Arms Inn (1844) has also been recently restored.

At Bridgewater we crossed the bridge on our way into Hobart. Still the jewel in Tasmania's crown, it is Australia's second oldest city after Sydney — and where else could we have found a blend of old and new so easy on the eye?

The port area has always fascinated me. I can still see those four-masters and blubber-slicked whaling vessels moored at Constitution Dock. Even today, the Japanese fishing fleet continues that long seafaring tradition one associates with Hobart. One-legged seagulls and old pubs lend a salty air to a city with a noble pedigree.

The last stop on our journey was Huonville, south of Hobart. Largest apple producing centre of Australia, the region itself was discovered by a Frenchman, Admiral d'Entrecasteaux, in 1792. He named the region after his second-in-command, Captain Huon de Kermandec.

Such is our island State, filled with green colours and gentility. Our pilgrimage south from Launceston through central Tasmania led us into some strange nooks in pursuit of the past. What we discovered, too, was the way in which Tasmanians accept their history as being part of the richness of their own lives.

Courtyard at Sandhill, Oatlands, a fine Georgian stone house built by James Bryant. The outbuildings include the two-storey brick stables, a coach house and a sheepdip carved from sandstone. Named by Governor Macquarie, the town of Oatlands reminded him of his native Scotland.

Rural landscapes, though drought-stricken, still hint at the subdued tonings of autumn.

Lake Dulverton near Oatlands
is a popular tourist spot. Old stone
buildings give an historic air to
this charming village.

107

Better known for its troubled convict background, Tasmania nevertheless is home to many of Australia's landed families. Though few remain on their estates today, the homesteads their forebears built reflect an anglicised vision of how the land should appear. John Glover, the famous landscape painter, portrayed Tasmania in a similar Picturesque fashion. A red-roofed farmhouse and quilted, rolling hills around Bothwell exemplify the countryside so admired by the early colonials.

Rural landscape near Bothwell.

❛ *Hobart Town scenery is beautiful, no doubt — never having seen it, I cannot speak of its merits — but, with a little trouble, Launceston and the surrounding country will disclose as much beauty as the most fastidious could wish for. The railway route by the Launceston and Western Railway, from Launceston to Deloraine, passes through some of the loveliest scenery in Northern Tasmania — undulating plains, beautified by man with arts taught by nature; golden grain uprearing its bearded heads; water courses, winding and nestling amidst over-hanging trees and verdant grasses; hills in the distance, cloud capped or green. All breathe of beauty, and form a grand picture of still life, rendered more attractive by the hand of nature-instructed man.* ❜

(New Chum (pseud.), A Ramble in Launceston, *Office of the 'Cornwall Chronicle', Launceston, 1879*)

Gardens setting and ivy walls contrasting with ornamental lakes reflect the strong English influence on the landscape near Hadspen.

Old stone buildings around Bagdad are a strong reminder of early English influence. Bagdad, like Jericho, was named by the early explorer, Hugh Germaine — an avid reader of the Bible and The Arabian Nights.
Of historical interest in the Bagdad region is Sayers Court homestead, built by Dr John Espie. The body of an Aboriginal shot on this property was, for many years, propped up by a spear under the chin and left in a hollow tree; such was the brutality of many of the early settlers towards the indigenous people.

Near Kempton, the land is undulating pastoral country with a history
reaching back to 1817 when Anthony Fenn Kemp took up a grant of land in the region.

OPPOSITE PAGE: *Convict-constructed
outbuilding near Kempton was once used as
living quarters. Further south, on the road
near Nile, a farmer returns home after
sorting his cattle.*

PRECEDING PAGE:
*Early colonial homestead on the road between
Campbelltown and Kempton.*

Around Evandale and Nile, rural activities are predominantly associated with the breeding of fat lambs and cattle.

A contrast in pub styles at Kempton. While it is difficult to imagine the more formal of the two buildings running out of beer, mischievous little people have been held responsible for less serious occurrences.

PRECEDING PAGE:
On the western side of the Derwent River is Constitution Dock, the major port facility for the city of Hobart. The main port area is built on Sullivan Cove, the site of the first settlement in 1804, and the town's history has been dominated by ocean-related industries such as sealing, whaling and shipbuilding. Even today, Hobart is known the world over for being the destination of the annual Sydney to Hobart Yacht Race.

Second oldest capital in Australia, Hobart was proclaimed a city in 1842. It was a whaling port for many years and so has had a long association with the sea. Lieutenant-Colonel David Collins founded Hobart in 1804 and named it in honour of Lord Hobart, then Imperial Secretary of State for the Colonies.

Hobart Town

❛ *Some of the gentlemen's houses are handsome and elegant, and possess everything to render the inhabitants comfortable. The rents are, however, very high, as a house with eight rooms lets for £80 per annum, and £200 per annum is not an uncommon rental for a house with twelve or thirteen apartments. "The view from the harbour", says Mr. Prinsep, "would make the most magnificent panorama in the world, were a painter to give the deep brown and purple tints to the foliage which clothe these hills; . . . most of the principal buildings are seen from the river, the chief part of the town itself being judiciously hid in the valley behind. Above are the gentlemen's houses, interspaced amongst the trees, and to the left of them, the quadrangle and flagstaff of the barracks. Behind lies a deep valley, from which rises the magnificent table mountain called Mount Wellington. It is about seven miles distant to the west, and nearly four thousand feet high. The atmosphere is so clear, that unless its sides are gracefully wreathed in clouds, I can distinguish very little ravine or undulation. It is covered with woods to the ledge of rugged rocks, which it bears aloft like a mural crown, emblematic of the future prosperity of the infant city!* ❜*

(Parker, H. W., The Rise, progress, and present state of Van Diemen's Land; with advice to emigrants.
Also, a chapter on convicts, showing the efficacy of transportation as a secondary punishment, J. Cross, London, 1822).*

Elegant houses and ordered gardens are a feature of Hobart. Imported milestones often created a familiar impression of the home country for early colonists.

OPPOSITE PAGE:

Modelled on the Royal Tennis Court in Haymarket, London, the Royal Tennis Court buildings in Hobart are the earliest known courts in Australia and are still in use today.

Huonville is one of the largest apple-producing regions of Australia. It was first discovered by the
French Admiral d'Entrecasteaux who named it after his second-in-command, Captain Huon de Kermandec.
Huonville is also an important commercial centre serving the surrounding townships of Glen Huon,
Judbury and Ranelagh.

It's Showtime

SYDNEY'S ROYAL EASTER SHOW

Some events in the national calendar lie at the very foundation of our collective psyche. Like a poem of Banjo Paterson's, many of us at one time or another in our lives have felt our hearts quicken in response to the knowledge that the Royal Easter Show is once more upon us. It is the one event of the year when the people of New South Wales celebrate the abundant produce of the land: how the Show fares, so fares New South Wales and, perhaps, even Australia.

My own memories of the Show, like those of most Sydneysiders, go back to the haze of childhood. To me, even now, it represents one long dream sequence of sample bags filled with surprises that, as children, we could not hope to buy ourselves.

Each year we all looked forward to Showtime in order to repeat the exhausting saga of the year before. Collecting sample bags in various anonymous pavilions, growing stickier by the hour amid whirls of pink fairyfloss, crawling over glimmering tractors or threshing machines in the hope of finding some loose nob to take home — all these images made up the event that other people, namely adults, called the Royal Easter Show.

OPPOSITE PAGE: *The lucky winner of the 1982 Cake Decorating Competition receives the blue-and-gold victory sash.*

133

Fizzy drinks, delectable food, sample bags, funny hats, a chat with a bull and a rest on the grass . . . the Royal Easter Show is a child's cornucopia.

135

No Easter Show is complete without sideshows and fun for the children. The sideshow area here has a noisy and colourful excitement of its own. Gaily painted merry-go-rounds, ferris wheels, boxing booths, dancing and singing troupes, wild west shows, big dippers, dodgem cars, shooting galleries and hooplas give the Easter Show its carnival air.

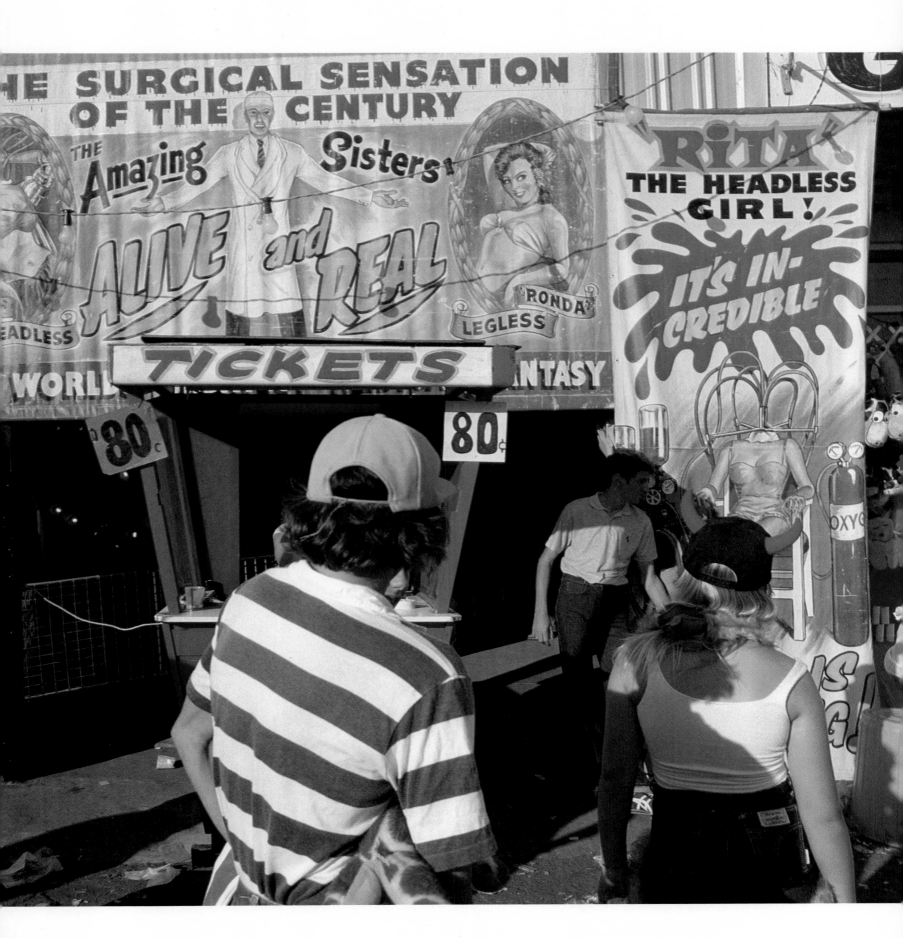

The Show

‘ *The big Show at Moore Park, its displays expanding year by year in numbers and varieties,*
tends increasingly to shed the character of an Agricultural Show and assume that of an exhibition.
While some find ground for objection in this transition, it is probably the best thing of its kind
that could happen, since it gives the State, and in no small degree Australasia, a representative
rallying-ground, and once a year focusses attention on the country's productivity and commerce . . .
The innumerable vocations of both town and country all have their places in a picture
wherein is assembled a little of the best of everything. ’

(The Daily Telegraph, Wednesday, April 15, 1908)

TODAY, tens of thousands of young Australians are still
introduced to their country via the Easter Show. The
journey to Moore Park is a child's pilgrimage whose goal
is the stimulation of sight, sound, smell and touch. We look
with bewilderment at stud bulls, watch horsemen crumble in
water jumps and stand around while giant pumpkins on tables
win prizes.

Yet there is a more prosaic side to the Easter Show. After
all, it does have a serious purpose. At agricultural fairs the
world over, people enjoy displaying their wares alongside
those of their peers. In New South Wales, every farmer worth
his salt would like to breed a show winner at least once in
his life.

Founded in 1822, the first show was held at Westmead,
near Parramatta. By all accounts it was a lively affair. A few
sheep were shown though by far the most popular exhibit was
the locally made beer. Between ploughing competitions and
jam tastings, many of the visitors partook of the amber fluid.
A newspaper commented: 'Reason was dethroned and folly
reigned in its stead.'

The food displays in the agricultural pavilion reflect long hours of work
arranging the fruit and vegetables in inventive designs.

Contemplating her preserved fruits, an exhibitor awaits the judge's verdict.

The Royal Agricultural Society finally settled in its present home in 1882 when it leased sixteen hectares of land from the City Council at a cost of $20 per annum. Boasting huge attendance figures over the years, the R.A.S. often rivalled Test Cricket as a crowd drawer. By 1947 over 1,500,000 people were going along each year.

With a charter to 'promote and encourage the development of the agricultural, pastoral, dairying, farmyard, viticultural, horticultural, mining and industrial resources of the State of N.S.W.', the R.A.S. has since broadened its base to include entertainment, product showings, rodeo contests, steer riding and camp draft contests to excite the crowd.

Even old Hilton Kenny, down from Boorowa this year with his prize bull, Jesmond Muffet, finds it a little bewildering. He's not getting any younger, nor is his Hereford bull. But Jesmond Muffet has already taken out a few local Grand Champion prizes around Boorowa, and Hilton is hoping for the same success in Sydney.

Many hopefuls each year come from near and far to show the very best of their flock, herd, crop or vegetable patch. The blue-and-gold victory sash, however, is about as attainable as Nirvana to a Buddhist monk. Yet still they enter, hoping that their Afghan hound or fantail pigeon will win that coveted prize.

The image of agricultural perfection has fascinated me since I was a child. Gazing at a stud merino then, its fleece combed to within an inch of its life, always managed to fill me with a sense of undisguised awe. My reasoning was that, if a sheep could be bred to appear so arrogantly perfect, what chance did I have surviving as I did in those days on bread and butter puddings and leftovers from the night before?

Still, that's showtime for us all: observing the land's yield in the mosaic form of melons, apricots, green apples and more helps to bring home to the layman how rewarding a farmer's life can sometimes be. Life on the land may suffer in times of drought, floods and bushfire but a farmer knows the pleasure of actually tasting the fruits of his own endeavour.

The cake decorating competition is just one of the many varied activities at the Easter Show.
The judges have a difficult task grading the contributions because of the great technical expertise and
the wealth of creativity exhibited.

142

❛ Mr. Walter Bradley asserted that he knew of a suitable area of land for a showground
and a committee was appointed to ascertain what sites were available... The result was that
the Society obtained a lease of 40 acres of common land on Moore Park. The piece of land
was very swampy and rocky and it is not wondered that the Council hesitated for some time before
taking the plunge and deciding to move to Moore Park... The first Show was held at Moore Park
at Easter, 1882 and ran for seven days. Gradually the ground was knocked into some kind of shape.
Thousands of loads of rubbish and street sweepings were dumped by the City Council
in the depressions, and some of these were filled from a depth of 14 feet... In October of 1891 it was
announced that Her Majesty, Queen Victoria, had granted an application for sanction to prefix
the word "Royal" to the name of the Agricultural Society of New South Wales...

For a number of years past the Council has pursued a steady policy based on the competitive
system and the education of the people in the value of primary production to the State. It would,
of course, be impossible to quote individual instances of the actual results of the competitive system,
but we have ample evidence that thousands of city dwellers and others, who have followed up
the Royal Shows, have been impelled by their comparative examinations of the products
of the soil to secure land and become producers in the country. ❜

(Somer, H. W., A Short History of The Royal Agricultural Society of New South Wales, 1922)

A poll Hereford stud bull 'goes up' for auction at the show.
Having received second prize in the judging, no doubt his price would have 'gone up' also.

An old timer knows when he's on a winner. His bull smells the blue ribbon even before he reaches the main show ring.

For those who compete, the business of winning can become as serious as making the land pay. Hilton Kenny tends Jesmond Muffet with all the attentive care that he might bestow on a wife, if he had one. Jesmond, great sire that he is, merely observes the world with his usual, rather beefy stare. Nothing ever fazes a champion, I soon learned.

'He's got a good bloodline, has J. M.,' Hilton confided to me in the stock showers. 'I bred him up out of tough Boorowa stock, I did.'

'Is that all it takes to produce a champion?' I asked.

'Oh nooo,' old Hilton Kenny breathed. His aging necktie remonstrated with the folds of flesh around his neck. 'You've got to make them believe they're champions, otherwise no amount of combing will pull them through.'

'And Jesmond Muffet is a champion.'

'He sure is. That animal has been through a lot to get here.'

'Judging by your hat, so have you, Hilton,' I said, slapping him affectionately on the shoulder.

The Royal Easter Show celebrates the continuing fecundity of the nation's land and livestock. Whether it's horses or dogs, cockerels or pigs, the parade is endless. You can watch wine being tasted or waiters racing, woodchoppers' axes glittering or rodeo riders tumbling. Bands play, soldiers march, stunt riders fling themselves through hoops of fire while children plummet earthward in a dipper of screams. Flags, bunting, tiered cakes and bottled fruit all compete for the spectator's glance.

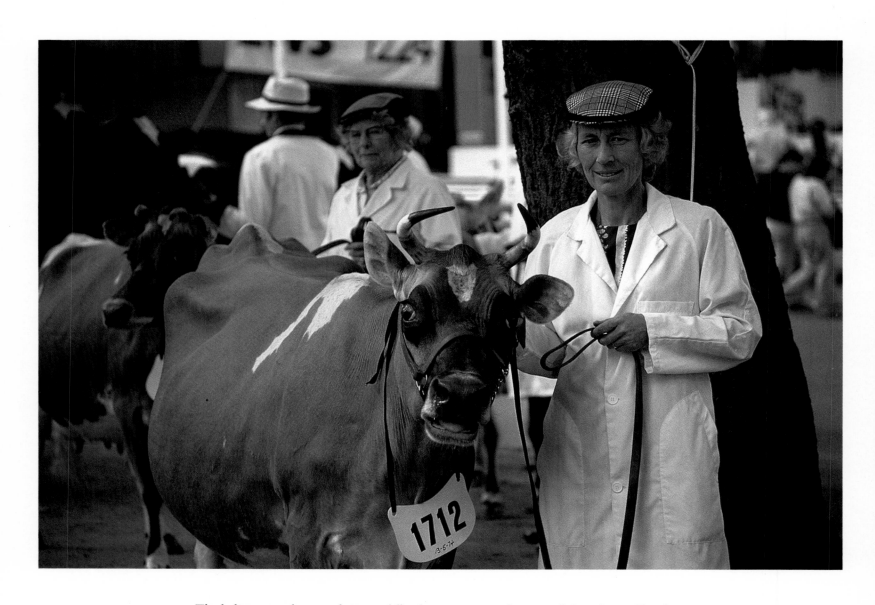

The ladies are as keen as their menfolk when it comes to showing off their deep-uddered cows.
Pampered aristocrats, these dairy cows are highly prized for their docile temperaments and milking qualities.

Six months or more goes into the showing of champions. It can be worth it: some beef bulls at the Show will be sold for over $10,000. Cleaning up before the main showing is like caring for babies and the judge has his work cut out picking a winner.

For the children, there is that other, more magical world to explore. Who hasn't come away from the Show with a vision of the Bearded Lady fixed firmly in the mind's eye? Or perhaps the memory of some oriental snake charmer, whose exotic tune has raised a squirming reptile from its wicker basket, lingers on. Then there's that belly dancer who continues to tantalise while holding on to her last veil. There's the nursery farm, too, for city children to experience the land on their own terms. They are allowed to touch and squeeze, cuddle a lamb in their arms and in so doing embrace their own understanding of Australia.

Above all, the Royal Easter Show is Australia's answer to a Wagner *Ring* opera at Beyreuth in Germany or the more traditional Trooping of the Colour. It's a truly indigenous event, one that has grown up out of the land itself. The Canadians may have their Calgary Stampede and the Americans their Texas State Fair, but none surpasses the greatest show on earth — New South Wales' Royal Easter Show.

'In any case, JM has been a good friend to me,' Hilton Kenny remarked as he led his bull back from the main show ring after missing out at the judging.

'What happened?' I asked.

'The judge noticed an old scar he got after a run-in with a barbed-wire fence,' the old man replied.

'That shouldn't have counted for too much.'

'It damned well won't when it comes to getting at those heifers back in the stock shower.' Hilton Kenny managed to raise a semblance of a smile. After all, showtime was over for him, at least until next year.

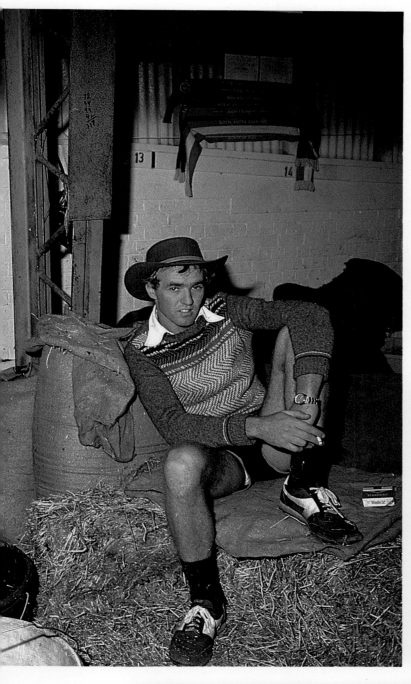

Life behind the glittering facade of the Show is very much like it is down on the farm. In rare moments man and beast are able to take a break. However, there are times when a good practical joke doesn't go astray. It would appear as if the Brahman bull finally took his revenge and has the keeper exactly where he wants him, so now he can rest in peace.

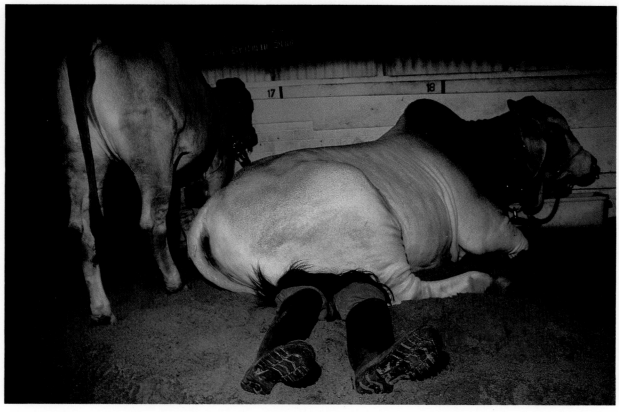

The horse has always been a part of the Australian ethos and at the Show there is no exception. Over two thousand horses compete each year in various classes, so washing them down before the big parade is an important job. Combing and plaiting a horse's tail is part of the star treatment.

Training a horse each day and putting it through its paces requires sensitivity and patience for, unlike many animals, horses are extremely responsive to the temperament of their trainers.

153

Horse showing is an important part of the Royal Easter Show and owners come from all over the State to exhibit in different categories. For the duration of the Show these animals enjoy the pampering they receive.

The Grand Parade. Rich in tradition, the competitors ride in ever-increasing circles before audience and judges alike. It's the one event that no-one wants to miss when the pride of Australia's livestock turns out in force. Forty thousand people from all over the world watch such regular features of the ring events as polo, show jumping, tent-pegging, trotting and sheep dog contests.

*The Grand Parade is helped along with a dash of colour from mounted police and ceremonial bands.
However, it is the procession of Grand Champions that reflects the Show's true purpose.*

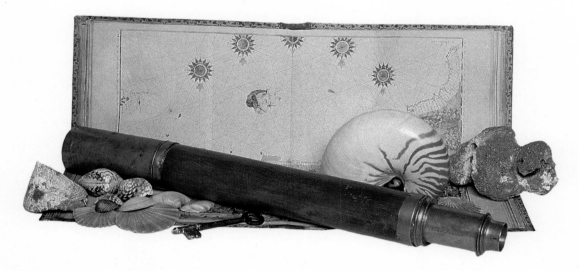

Looking for the Mahogany Ship

THE GRAMPIANS AND SOUTH COAST OF VICTORIA

Setting out to find the wreck of an ancient ship requires
a great deal of patience, I discovered, particularly when it lies buried under
several thousand tonnes of sand. However, when this ship may hold the
secret to the names of the first seafarers ever to have set foot on Australian soil,
then the quest can become more than just a treasure hunt.

The wreck of an early 16th century Portuguese caravel certainly exists
and is buried under a mountain of sand on a windswept beach somewhere
along the southern coast of Victoria, between Port Fairy and Warrnambool.

The story tells how Cristovão de Mendonça, commander of a fleet
of three fighting caravels out of Goa, sailed along this stretch of coastline
sometime around 1522. No one knows for sure what he was doing
in this remote part of the world but conjecture has it that he was trying to
intercept Magellan on his globe-encircling voyage. One thing we do know
is that a storm or tidal wave raging up from the Antarctic washed one of
his ships high up onto the beach.

The 'Mahogany Ship', as it was later named, was re-discovered
in 1826 by a couple of Tasmanian sealers. Their boat had overturned in
a nearby river estuary west of Warrnambool. Setting out to walk along the
beach towards the small sealers' depot at Port Fairy, they were suddenly
confronted by the stark outline of a shipwreck lying high on the beach.

Since then, like some half-mythical vessel, the Mahogany Ship has
disappeared as often as it has appeared. The sand dunes have shifted over the
years, burying the sun-whitened wreck once more; it was last seen in 1880.

OPPOSITE PAGE: *The high, flat coastal plains of Port Campbell National
Park have been eroded into fantastic formations by the actions of heavy
seas. Sheer cliffs rise up to ninety metres and natural archways,
caves, grottos, and blowholes abound.*

THE idea that Australia may have been discovered first by the Portuguese and not the Dutch seemed to me to be an interesting prospect. I wondered at the notion of our existing kangaroo and emu coat-of-arms being enhanced by the incorporation of the Rose of Portugal.

So we made the journey south to the coast through the Grampians. This rugged sandstone range of mountains forms the western rampart of the Great Dividing Range and was named by the explorer Major Thomas Mitchell who mistakenly described them as 'the extreme summits of the Southern Hemisphere'. One of the most beautiful and diverse habitats for native vegetation in Victoria, the Grampians are the home of Victoria's floral emblem, the common heath (*Epacris impressa*), which blooms all year round.

Over one hundred species of native orchids and some two hundred bird species also inhabit the timeless escarpments of this mountainous region. Crimson rosellas, honeyeaters and yellow-tailed black cockatoos are only some of the birds that haunt the great ferns and cassinias growing among the moist gullies. Forests, lakes and mist-shrouded waterfalls, too, lend a mysterious, almost primordial quality to the ancient landscape. The natural shelter of the terrain also provides an ideal habitat for kangaroos and koalas.

However, we had come south to explore the surf-slicked beaches and windswept promontories of the coast. Standing on the deck of his ship, Cristovão de Mendonça must have wondered whether he had voyaged to the very limits of the earth as he gazed at the eroded limestone cliffs before him.

The coastline is part of Port Campbell National Park. Its 32 km of seashore is peppered with caves, archways and a myriad of islands. Between 1855 and 1908 five ships were wrecked during storms along the park's coastline. The worst of these shipwrecks occurred in 1878 when the three-masted iron clipper *Loch Ard* went down, resulting in the loss of fifty lives.

Today, the park offers a fascinating range of coastal landforms with natural bridges and rock stacks. Best known of these are London Bridge, the Haystack, Marble Arch and the Twelve Apostles. Such coastal outcrops form a natural sanctuary for many species of seabirds: sheerwaters and fairy penguin colonies breed on the promontories and beaches.

PRECEDING SIX PAGES AND ABOVE:
Pages 164-171. East of Port Campbell are the rugged majesty of London Bridge and innumerable rock buttresses that include the Twelve Apostles. The outcrops form a natural sanctuary for many species of seabirds.

❝ *The unknown dead who manned this vessel and who, like Balboa, might have claimed*
our water 'for Rome, for Leon, for Castille', I believe were the first navigators who saw our shores.
After them, till the commencement of this century, 'the long wash of Australasian seas on our
southern coasts were never gazed on by civilised man'. ❞

(Mr Julian Thomas ["The Vagabond"], quoted in Archibald, J., 'Notes on the ancient wreck discovered near Warrnambool',
The Argus, 10th November, 1884 and read before the 20th Ordinary General Meeting of the Royal Geological Society for Australasia)

The rugged coastline is punctuated with small villages like Apollo Bay. Apollo Bay began life as a whaling settlement called Middleton in 1854 but it later was gazetted as Krambruk, an Aboriginal name for a sandy place. Only in 1952 did the popular local name for the bay become the official name for the town.

Apollo Bay, further east beyond Cape Otway and cossetted among rolling downs that reach to the water's edge, is a small fishing village reminiscent of a smuggler's cove in some English children's book. Fishermen's graves stand on the hill, facing towards the southern ocean and behind them the picturesque green hills are home to flocks of sheep.

Over one hundred kilometres to the east is Corio Bay where Governor La Trobe was present, in 1847, when a set of antique keys were found some seven metres underground, at the bottom of a recently excavated lime-kiln.

The keys were of extremely early design and unlike any that Governor La Trobe had ever seen before. It was possible that they had been inadvertently dropped on the beach long ago by one of Cristovão de Mendonça's crew while replenishing their water supplies. Although the Geelong Keys, as they are now known, have since been lost, they represent a real clue to the whereabouts of the Mahogany Ship.

We travelled westward then, to Warrnambool and Port Fairy. Originally an early whaling station, Port Fairy developed quickly as a coastal trading port after 1840. Later, it became an important fishing port. A feature of the town is its bluestone cottages erected in the middle of last century. Once more the salt air was blowing on our faces. Wandering down the quaint old streets of Port Fairy, past early pubs such as the Stag Hotel and the Merrijig Inn, we sensed the town's long seafaring tradition. Indeed, we half expected to see old men in doorways, sucking on their briar pipes.

‘ *I was working with my knife, to detach some of the shells, when the lime-burner joined us.
On seeing how I was engaged, and overhearing the conversation with my companion, he said, ‘I found
a bunch of keys yesterday, just where your honour is picking the shells.’ ‘Keys?’ I said.
‘Keys, your honour,’ he replied. ‘What can you mean?’ I enquired. ‘Yes, here,’ he said, laying
his hand just upon the shellbed. I asked him ‘Where are they?’ ‘Up at the hut, your honour,’ he
replied. ‘Let me see them,’ I said. He immediately left the excavation and ran up the bank
to his hut, returning a minute or two afterwards with two keys, each about two inches in length,
which he handed to me, saying that there had been three, but that the children had been playing
with them, and he could only lay his hand upon the two.* ’*

(from a conversation between Alexander Mollison and Governor LaTrobe as reported by Mr T. Rawlinson
in a paper delivered to the Royal Society of Victoria circa 1875)*

Kolor homestead is a single storey, Classical Revival construction built in 1868. It was designed by Joseph Reed for the Irish-born pastoralist, John Twomey, whose wealth extended to the embellishment of a tower over the entry portico.

Once in Warrnambool we knew that we were getting closer to the Mahogany Ship for it was not far from here, on a lonely stretch of beach washed by a sea that extends as far south as the Patagonian Peninsula in South America, that one of Cristovão de Medonça's caravels was swept shoreward one stormy day. We know it was here because the famous Rotz map drawn by his cartographers stops at this point.

Captain John Mason, a long-time resident of the region, stumbled upon the wreck in the summer of 1846 while riding along the beach from Port Fairy to Warrnambool. He later wrote: 'My attention was attracted to the hull of a vessel embedded high and dry in the hummocks, far above the reach of the tide . . .' He went on to describe the wreck as 'a vessel of about 100 tons burden, and from its bleached and weather-beaten appearance must have been there many years. The spars and deck were gone, and the hull full of drift sand. The timber of which she was built had the appearance of either mahogany or cedar.'

So a legend was born. The elusive Mahogany Ship lives on under a natural sarcophagus of sand. No one has yet been fortunate enough to re-discover that 'hull full of drift sand', least of all ourselves. However, like most sunken treasures, it will always be there for someone who wants to make the journey through the Grampians and down to this wind-blasted stretch of coastline.

Perhaps the next person will be luckier than we were. He may discover some relic, perhaps a shell-brined Portuguese coin up there in the dunes where, I'm sure, Cristovão de Mendonça's lost caravel still lies.

174

Relics of the earliest days of settlement in the Port Campbell region abound. Near Port Campbell itself is the cemetery that commemorates the tragedy of the Loch Ard; the head-stones loom out of a cleared patch of windblown coastal scrub, a constant reminder of the merciless coastline that sent the Mahogany Ship down to its grave. Despite setbacks in the 1840s prosperous landowners played an important part in the development of the region. Many of the homesteads and mansions in the area reflect early colonial tastes.

175

The Great Ocean Road linking Wye River and Apollo Bay was built before WWI and is a remarkable feat of engineering even today. The road allows visitors to view some exceptional coastal scenery. Cattle graze down as far as the headlands above deserted beaches near Apollo Bay but, only a few kilometres inland, the country changes into farming land characteristic of Australian dairying country.

Sheep, dairy cattle and crops all flourish in the Western
District around Port Campbell. It was first discovered by
Major Thomas T. Mitchell in 1836 although the
Henty brothers had already settled at Portland some two years
earlier. With Mitchell's discovery of fertile land, many
settlers arrived from Tasmania, Sydney and particularly the
Scottish lowlands to share in the Henty's prosperity.
To this day the Western District remembers its early pastoral
beginnings by naming the local Commonwealth
electoral district Henty.

PRECEDING FOUR PAGES:
Pages 178-181. The sleepy dairying settlements
of Ferguson and Beach Forest lie between Apollo Bay and
Lavers Hill. Nearby clear streams provide a picturesque
setting among secluded hills.

183

Rising from the surrounding plains to peaks
that appear far higher than a thousand metres, the
Grampians form the western end of the
Great Dividing Range and cover an area of
220,000 hectares. Lake Victoria, a man-made
lake, provides an ideal sanctuary for wildlife
in the region. An abandoned stockyard in a
stand of ghostly conifers reminds us of early
pioneering days.

PRECEDING PAGE:
The Balconies are part of the spectacular
rock escarpments of the saw-toothed mountain
range known as the Grampians. A steep climb
to The Balconies is rewarded with the view
of this rugged volcanic region.

Gateway to the Grampians, Mount Abrupt dominates the tiny hamlet of Dunkeld.

Reed beds in Lake Victoria provide a haven for numerous species of waterfowl.

PRECEDING PAGE:
Mackenzie Falls in the Grampians formed as a result of a geological upheaval that severely tilted the whole range.

View of Lake Victoria at dusk from the Balconies.

Early morning view from the Grampians looking towards Port Campbell.

At places like Moorfield Park, near Geelong, deer are raised to satisfy the growing demand for venison. Special high fences are required to enclose herds, particularly during the mating season.

FOLLOWING PAGE:
Zumstein, an old German hermit, regularly fed the kangaroos until his death. Today kangaroos can still be fed by hand.

193

All Things German

TOWNS IN SOUTH AUSTRALIA

On a hill overlooking the vine-green Barossa Valley stands a mere leaf of a town called Bethany, the birthplace of German settlement in Australia. Bethany is one of the few examples outside Germany of what is known as *Waldhufendorf* — a German forest village dating from the reign of Charlemagne in the 9th century. Such is the sense of history that pervades this valley in the Mount Lofty Ranges; even today, a unique culture still manages to survive.

Born from a need to escape religious persecution in Germany back in the 1840s, a tiny band of God-fearing Lutherans migrated to Australia to a place they named *das Barossa Tal*. To them it was indeed Shangri-la, the lost valley. They worked hard ploughing the land, initially as subsistence farmers under the guiding hand of George Fife Angas, a prominent local landowner and founder of the South Australian Company. It was he that encouraged them to come out to Australia and found their settlements.

Soon, more towns sprung up until the valley rang to the sound of such German names as Kaiser Stuhl, Tanunda and even a river christened the Rhine. Vines were originally planted in 1847 at Jacob's Creek by a Silesian farmer, Johann Gramp. Three years later he bottled his own vintage — a white wine of the hock type. He was soon followed by others — men such as Joseph Gilbert at Pewsey Vale, Samuel Hoffman near Tanunda and Joseph Seppelt at Seppeltsfield.

OPPOSITE PAGE: Wine barrels grace the cellars at Saltram winery in Angaston. Angaston took its name from George Fife Angas and his family home of Collingrove was, until recently, occupied by Angas' descendants. In 1976, however, the home was given to the National Trust.

SOUTH
AUSTRALIA

Barossa
Valley

In the old settlement of Bethany is a former shepherd's cottage, called Landhaus, which was built in the 1850s and has been restored to its original style. Landhaus has made Bethany famous for another reason than its historical significance for it has become Australia's smallest motel, catering for two guests at a time.

TODAY, more than thirty Barossa Valley wineries testify to the vision of those early German pioneers. While they were busy building their Lutheran churches, they were equally busy creating one of the nation's most important industries. The clear, Mediterranean skies and crisp winters made the region ideal for producing vintage wines.

The skills of the Barossa wine makers are often hereditary. In many wineries we encountered men tending vines planted by their great grandfathers. In fact, John Menge, a well known vintner that we met in the valley, was quick to indicate his own background even though he was not aware of doing so as he spoke.

'Sure, my great grandfather came out here with the first batch of Settlers,' he said.

PRECEDING FOUR PAGES:
Pages 198/199: The first German settlement in the Valley occurred at Bethany in 1842. Bethany Reserve, around which many of the early settlers lived, is still ringed with some of their early cottages.
Pages 200/201: The country around Keyneton is usually the epitome of peace and tranquillity, until late summer when the entire Valley becomes enveloped in the frenetic, round-the-clock activity of grape-picking, carting, crushing and storing.

'I suppose now you only live for the grape, is that it, John?'

'But of course! There is nothing more satisfying in life than a glass of wine.' He smiled as he thrust a glass of riesling across the table towards me. 'Try this,' he added.

I sipped the almost clear, oak-flavoured wine.

'Is that not better than life itself?' John Menge inquired. That smile of his, I noticed, had become almost beatific.

You can't hurry a fine wine and we discovered that these hill towns of South Australia expect to be savoured just as slowly. At the geographic centre of the Barossa Valley lies the town of Tanunda. Tanunda boasts a number of fine Gothic Revival churches such as Langmeil Lutheran; Pastor Kavel, the founder of the Lutheran Church in Australia is buried nearby. The town also has a number of well preserved German cottages built around Goat Square, near where the original marketplace once stood.

Other townships welcome you with their smile. One of my favourites is Angaston, home of Saltram's Wines and the Angas family, not to mention my father. The town is stolidly British, with an air of robust nationalism about it. In this respect, I can recall a story told about my father when he was a small boy. Whenever he heard *God Save the King* being played at night in the church across the road, it was said of him that he would always climb out of bed and stand rigidly to attention in his multi-striped pyjamas.

*Around Keyneton the Valley's land is not wasted: besides vineyards
the land is used for cropping and sheep raising.*

Whatever else might be said about the Barossa Valley and neighbouring hill towns, the most apparent feature is the fine balance that exists between church spire and patch-worked fields. At a glance one can appreciate the almost Germanic obsession for clear definition between farmland and common. The towns seem to be spread neatly about, much as if they were a part of the Rhineland.

Yalumba and Oakbank offer interesting contrasts in architectural styles. The stonework, for example, on a winery wall in Yalumba has none of the embroidery of richer estates in the region. Solid stonework harks back to a time when men expected the results of their industry to remain long after they had gone.

Indeed, a strong sense of craftsmanship was a feature of all the wood and stonework that we encountered. Whether it was an American oak wine barrel or a row of vines stretching over a hill, I think that we always knew that this feeling for precision — not only of line but of conception — had been the hallmark of those early craftsmen's work.

Hahndorf is perhaps best known of all the South Australian hill towns. Situated east of Adelaide, deep in the Mount Lofty Ranges, Hahndorf was once an important staging post between the capital and Murray Bridge on the Murray River. Goods and provisions passed through Hahndorf on bullock teams bound for the great paddlesteamer port and points north along the river.

Seppeltsfield winery was founded by Joseph Seppelt, a Silesian migrant who purchased the land in 1852 in order to grow tobacco. The winery is almost a village in itself, housing both main and storage buildings constructed of bluestone and surrounded by landscaped gardens and picnic areas. The grand entrance to Seppeltsfield, flanked by date palms planted in the Great Depression to maintain employment, is a feature of the landscape.

The Yalumba winery at Angaston was established by Samuel Smith in 1849. Features of the two-storey building, constructed of blue marble, are the castellated tower, the clock tower and courtyard. Yalumba is surrounded by attractive gardens.

Wine tasting is part of the way of life in the Barossa Valley and visitors to the region become equally as involved as the locals. They savour some of Australia's finest clarets and rieslings as well as a huge array of ports, sherries, sparkling wines and more.

Many of the old cottages in Hahndorf are inhabited by a variety of artists and craftsmen.

Today, Hahndorf is a popular tourist haven but this does not detract from the evident highlights of the place. You can still find the traditional bakery where bread is baked in true German style and the houses unabashedly reflect the popular half-timbered style of German provincial architecture. The Old Mill restaurant, built in 1864, was formally run as a flour mill by F. Wittwer and later his three sons, August, Wilhelm and Heinrich, before it was turned into a wool store.

Putlands Cottage, dating to 1840, is constructed of hand-made bricks, pegged beams and mud ceilings. Like many of the houses in Hahndorf it is a rather humble abode, built by men and women intent on fulfilling the least pretentious of dreams — simply to have a roof over their heads.

Such a sentiment probably reflects more exactly than any other the true flavour of the Barossa Valley and Adelaide hill towns. While there may be many stately country estates lying half-concealed behind tall stands of trees, the prevailing impression will remain one of Protestant rectitude and order.

The Burgermeister, or mayor, of Hahndorf is a living example of the emphasis on maintaining German tradition in the area. The beautiful countryside of Hahndorf was made famous by Sir Hans Heysen who lived in the town and attracted other artists to the area.

❝ *Tucked away in the heart of the Adelaide hills lies the quaint and quiet little town of Hahndorf, so old-world in its features that were it not for its southern setting one might fancy oneself transported into some little "dorf" of the German fatherland.*

The founding of the village dates back some 70 years, when 208 emigrants from Prussia landed in South Australia from the ship Zebra, commanded by Captain Hahn . . .

Captain Hahn proved himself a good leader. Land was found for the little band under his care in one of the fertile valleys of the Mount Barker ranges, and here the resourceful captain laid out the town which bears in his honour the name of Hahndorf . . .

The primitive shelters soon gave place to more substantial homes, all built after the manner of those that had been left behind in the homeland — high-gabled and roofed with thatch, and the old-fashioned straw-covered barns with the bake-ovens built like huge ant-hills some distance away from the house . . . even now, after a lapse of more than a century, Hahndorf retains for the most part the characteristics of a German village. The people still speak their native tongue, and the primitive methods of agriculture are still in vogue. One sees the good frau in the fields working like a man (it is the frau who does most of the work on a small holding, while the husband is occupied at a trade in the village or on the farms of larger landowners). The woman, in addition to the little troop of white-haired, blue-eyed children who claim her attention, has the charge of field and barn and house, and most capably does she fulfil her manifold duties. ❞

(H. Heysen, 'A German-Australian Village', The Lone Hand, June 1908, pages 194-197)

The gallery and museum in Hahndorf was once known as the Hahndorf Academy. Between 1857 and 1886, the Academy was an important local source of bilingual, post-primary education for children of German parents. The years may pass but in the twentieth century Hahndorf still remembers its past with pride — a penny farthing bicycle mounted on a store wall is indicative of that sense of history.

PRECEDING FOUR PAGES:
Page 210/211: Some Hahndorf cottages date back to the 1840s. The half-timbered style was typical of the period.
Page 212/213: Otto and his wife keep the German tradition of good food alive by baking mouthwatering German breads, cakes and pastries in their bakery.

There are numerous restaurants in Hahndorf. The Old Mill Restaurant has occupied Wittwer's flour mill (built in 1864) since 1971 when it was restored. Coffee houses cater to the passing tourist trade.

The Mount Lofty Ranges, which form a beautiful backdrop to Hahndorf, initially attracted timber cutters to the region early last century. The fertile land, though, gave the Germans the impetus to settle and farm the land rather than to supply building materials for the burgeoning town of Adelaide. Today the farming life continues with little to indicate that a century has passed.

PRECEDING PAGE: Houses such as the historic country estate at Oakbank, in the Mount Lofty Ranges, reflect an elegant lifestyle that is now almost impossible to maintain.

❛ . . . thus the villagers lead a happy and independent life, and by their sobriety, industry,
and general exemplary conduct, hold out a good example to all the other Colonists . . . These
Germans are the most persevering Colonists South Australia can boast of. They are possessed of
a plodding industry and a contented disposition, which enables them to put up with many
inconveniences at which English settlers would grumble, and though not so energetic as English
emigrants, they are better qualified for undergoing the hardships of a first settlement.
I used to take a pleasure in visiting their villages from time to time, to watch the slow but steady
progress they made . . . ere I left the Colony many of them had got respectable looking drays, with
a good horse or a couple of bullocks to drag them. Thus these men who began with almost
nothing, have got in Klemzig alone 150 head of cattle, 40 horses and ponies, and had in 1841, under
cultivation, 167 acres of wheat, 56 acres of barley, 10 acres of oats, and several acres
of potatoes, besides numerous gardens. ❜

(Bennett, J. F., Historical and descriptive account of South Australia: founded on the experience of
a Three Years' Residence in that Colony, *Smith, Elder & Co., Cornhill*, London, 1843, page 133)

A tree has all but overgrown the facade of the old stone church at Oakbank.
In Bethany, headstones mark the final resting place of early residents in the town
while, at Charleston, a more recent memorial is Centennial Park which
was established as a tribute to early German settlers. In yet another town, Tanunda,
is Langmeil Lutheran Church, almost concealed by a corridor of cypress trees.
The cemetery nearby is the last resting place of Pastor Kavel, not only the founder of
Bethany but also the father of the Lutheran Church in Australia. The church
itself was built in 1888 in the Gothic Revival style, using the local random
bluestone construction.

Tanunda is the Barossa Valley's geographic centre and is the town most closely associated with distinctly German characteristics. Places like Coffee Cottage and Goat Square give Tanunda an atmosphere all its own. Goat Square was the early settlers' first common. Another way of lending the area character is the placement of unusual garden ornaments, such as those seen dotted around the towns of the Mt Pleasant region.

222

*The Barossa Valley also has links with England and Spain. Colonel Light, South Australia's first
Surveyor-General, named the Valley after Barrosa, near Spain's sherry-producing district. All the towns of the Valley
are in its tiny confines — twenty-nine kilometres long and eight kilometres wide.*

Pewter Plate Country

EARLY SETTLEMENT IN WESTERN AUSTRALIA

No-one knows exactly how many Dutch East Indiaman ships have been wrecked off the Western Australian coast but these hulks are the last link between Western Australia and the European post-Renaissance seafaring tradition. Forsaking the silver bullion and valuable artefacts that sank to the bottom of the sea, shipwrecked sailors who made it to shore were reported to have changed their minds about divine providence when they encountered the dry and forbidding coastline of the Houtman or Abrolhos Islands off the coast near Geraldton. Survival seemed impossible and so it was a race against time to build an open boat that might permit a successful escape northwards to the East Indies.

Thus the State was rather reluctantly peopled for a time by shipwrecked sailors, long before New South Wales was proclaimed in the name of England by Governor Arthur Phillip and long before, in 1829, the remaining part of New Holland, now known as Western Australia, was also formally annexed. A tiny settlement eventually struggled into existence on the Swan River in 1829, under the command of Governor James Stirling. People sailed out from England to begin new lives on the western shores — and later the Avon Valley and Geraldton — little realising how foul were the moods of the weather that had already sent many a Dutchman to his grave.

OPPOSITE PAGE: *Near Geraldton, Western Australia, are the ruins of many settlers' cottages. Using the natural stone of the region, pioneers from England's North Country employed techniques that had served them well for centuries.*

WESTERN AUSTRALIA

Geraldton

Avon Valley

Ensign Dale crossed the Darling Ranges during the winter
of 1830 and discovered the fertile Avon Valley around York.
Governor Stirling later named the region Yorkshire on
the recommendation of the first settlers.

The town of York nestles at the foot of a hill and
has a distinctively English atmosphere
representative of the rustic, old-world charm of
the Avon Valley.

PRECEDING FOUR PAGES:
Pages 226-229: The rolling downs around Geraldton were considered by drought-stricken Avon Valley farmers to be fine farming
country. They ignored Captain King's pessimistic report, made
after journeying by ship along the coast in 1822, that the region
was hopelessly sterile.

St Patrick's Roman Catholic Church in York was built around 1848, just eighteen years after the settlement was founded.

THE settlers came with dreams of political and social experiment, hoping to separate themselves from the British systems of economics and land ownership. Allocated land, they proceeded to work much as they had done in England.

The barrier of the Darling Ranges was broken in the winter of 1830 when Ensign Dale crossed over and found the fertile land of the Avon Valley beyond. The country reminded the settlers so much of their homeland that Governor Stirling named the region Yorkshire. The first inland settlement in Western Australia began amidst optimism and early prosperity at a place called York. By 1836, Toodyay was also established.

Originally named Newcastle, Toodyay later had its name changed in order to avoid confusion with the New South Wales town of the same name. 'Toodyay' is a corruption of an Aboriginal word meaning a place of plenty, and is a reflection of the early settlers' attitude and hope for the future. Northam and Beverley, like Toodyay, all reflect that quiet, provincial air of England's North Country. Today, these towns support the important central wheat belt that stretches across the Avon Valley. However, those early halcyon days did not continue uninterrupted.

‘ *Nestling cosily in a valley through which the Avon River winds its sinuous course, and distant some sixty miles in an easterly direction from Perth, is the picturesque town of York, the centre of a great wheat-growing district of Western Australia. The town is one of the oldest-established settlements in the state, and there is an appearance of stability about it which is reassuring . . . In common with the rest of the agricultural districts, the production of the country in the vicinity of York has vastly increased since the markets, which were established on the discovery of the eastern goldfields, have been available for the disposal of agricultural produce . . . The streets of York are wide and well made. Many of the buildings are of stone, notably the Roman Catholic and Wesleyan churches; while the local banks are also handsome structures. As is the case in all the older towns of the state, there are to be seen side by side old-fashioned buildings erected in the early days and handsome structures of modern design.* ’*

(Thiel, P. W. H. & Co., Twentieth Century Impressions of Western Australia, 1901, pages 736-737)

Initially, Avon Valley farmers were optimistic about their ability to manage the land, working long hours to establish property and livestock.

The old store at Greenough is a simple, rectangular stone building typical of those that flourished last century from the Avon to the Murchison.

PRECEDING PAGE:
Following the founding of the Swan River colony in 1829, the European settlers were anxious to find better agricultural land. Within a year, York, the first inland town of Western Australia, was founded. Towns like Toodyay, Beverley and Northam were later developed to serve the growing rural community.

The Avon Valley settlers failed to account for the variable weather cycles of the region and by the middle of the century, just as permanent buildings and prosperity began to grace the region, the first severe droughts blighted the attempts to civilise the country. So devastating were the perpetually rainless seasons that hundreds of settlers were forced to abandon their properties forever. They took to the few roads in the colony and began a trek northwards, driving what remained of their sheep flocks before them, in the search for more reliable pasture land.

An expedition of settlers finally reached the Murchison Basin at the site of Geraldton in 1854 but they were not the first Europeans to have visited the area. In 1629 the *Batavia* sank off the coast here and the next recorded contact was made in 1822. In that year, Captain Phillip Parker King noted in his diary the visit he made to the now legendary spot where Dirk Hartog, the Dutch navigator, nailed a pewter plate to a post on the beach:

> *We saw enough of it, however, to be convinced of its perfect sterility. The coast is lined with a barrier of rocks, on which the sea was breaking high, with a roar that was heard on board, although our distance from the shore was at least three miles.*

A few years later, in 1839, Lieutenant George Grey (later to become the Governor of South Australia and of New Zealand), together with a party of twelve men, was shipwrecked at Gantheaume Bay near the mouth of the Murchison River. They were forced to return on foot to Perth and on the trek southwards suffered terrible privations, including the loss of one young man through starvation.

An abandoned settler's cottage near Geraldton.

— Old Landmarks —

❛ *Studying Western Australian geography with the aid of a map is instructive and entertaining,
though notes of numerous wrecks tell an eloquent tale of the treacherous coast, bad luck, and
sometimes bad other things. Before we reach Geraldton . . . off Point Cloates — where
our vessel struggled gamely on a tempestuous Sunday night, which nervous passengers remembered
with the consoling thought that brethren and sisters on shore were, or ought to be, offering petitions
"for those in peril on the sea" — the Perth (formerly the Penola) came to grief in 1887, and
another foreign steamer, a few weeks before we reached the place . . . A feature of the industries
associated with Geraldton is the collection of guano in an extremely interesting locality,
and I regretted to have to decline a courteous invitation to visit the source of supply, an island
of the Abrolhos Group, about 40 miles from the town . . . These De Houtman Abrolhos Islands are
named after a fine plucky old Dutch mariner, who was 300 years ago Governor of Amboyna,
in the Malay Archipelago. Like most of the Netherlands navigators of the time, who discovered many
lands, but took possession of none, he sent out expedition after expedition, mainly for
honour and glory. In 1619 De Houtman, with 11 ships, appeared on the Abrolhos Reef, or Rocks,
and did what is suggested by the name which he gave to the place, "Keep your eyes open!"
That is what modern mariners have to do every day and every night in these latitudes, for
the coast is one of the most dangerous and the least clearly defined in Australasia.* ❜

(Sowden, W. J., 'With the nor'-west mail', The Adelaide Observer, April-May, 1903)

Australia's flightless bird, the emu, resembles the ostrich — its genuine counterpart both in behaviour and appearance.

Only a few years later, just before the full onslaught of the droughts were felt in the Avon Valley, lead was discovered on the Murchison River. The settlement that grew up to support the young mining enterprise became known as Gerald Town in honour of the new Governor Fitzgerald. The Avon Valley drought refugees soon began arriving overland with their sheep. When a jetty was constructed at Geraldton in 1860 in order to aid the expanding mining industry, the farmers later arrived by boat, bringing their flocks with them. Thus Geraldton began operating as a wool port as well as a port for the lead mining, until gold was discovered at Dawn and Mt Magnet in the 1890s.

One of the most significant buildings in Western Australia was built in Geraldton between 1916 and 1938. St Francis Xavier Cathedral was the brainchild of the remarkable Monsignor John Cyril Hawes. Monsignor Hawes had studied architecture in London and later practised his profession for fifteen years. After entering the priesthood, he was posted to Geraldton where, in the clear light of the south, he sought to build a cathedral of unique architectural character. He was impressed by the climate that reminded him so much of the Romanesque heartland of Spain and proceeded to design a building of harmonious proportion and mass. The twin-towered structure embodies Romanesque, Norman and Renaissance elements and, like much Spanish Colonial architecture, is built in random freestyle stone.

Further to the north of Geraldton, the coastal cliffs of Kalbarri are silent witnesses to those Dutch ships that were wrecked here during 17th century storms. On one of the islands offshore, the *Batavia* foundered in 1629. The captain sailed north to the East Indies in an open boat, hoping to obtain help. On his safe return he was angered to discover that, in his absence, some members of his crew had mutinied and killed many of the remaining crew members. He had the mutineers rounded up, tortured and later hanged for their misdeeds.

Early settlers of the Avon Valley failed to adapt quickly to the erratic weather patterns of the region and when faced with the onslaught of drought, headed north in search of greener pastures.

The former Dominican Convent, near the Geraldton Highway, is located in the hamlet of Greenough. Greenough contains many historic buildings which reflect the sturdy building techniques of those early pioneers.

PRECEDING PAGE:
Although no longer in use, the old Northam railway station still stands. In the busy days when the railway was being pushed through to the western goldfields, steam locomotives constantly chugged through Northam. One of the engines has been restored and stands near the old station.

Greenough is another town on the coast steeped in the State's colonial past. Like Geraldton, it was originally populated by Avon Valley farmers escaping the droughts down south. Small acre farms of 20 acres were quickly surveyed and by the 1860s Clinch's Mill had already been built to process the grain from record wheat harvests.

Using materials at hand, the people of Greenough constructed their houses and town buildings in a way that even today reflect a homespun, earthy quality. A walk around this remote country town somehow calls to mind a north country village in England.

The Geraldton region and Avon Valley are two areas of Western Australia that are quite different from one another. And yet they are linked by the accident of weather. Droughts caused migration from the Avon Valley to the Geraldton region and storms left shipwrecked sailors on the coast in both areas.

If those sailors had survived, how many more pewter plates would they have left for those Avon Valley farmers to discover?

The Grand Hotel in Northam has housed many railway travellers; Northam is a major rail centre in the Avon Valley and has lines from the eastern States and Kalgoorlie passing through its station. Just outside the town is Muresk College, the main agricultural college of the valley. The differences between the Swan and Avon Rivers do not end with the agricultural value of the land. In contrast to Perth, famous for its black swans, Northam has a population of white swans that make their home on the tree-lined banks of the Avon River. The swans were a gift of Northam's English namesake.

The first European actually to pass through the Greenough region was George Grey in 1839. By 1845, Avon Valley settlers, short of pasture following serious droughts, were pressing for exploration of the north-west on the basis of Grey's summation of the area. By 1859, the entire Greenough Shire was occupied by small farms. Today the ground pattern of many of the pioneers' houses can still be seen. Buildings were generally constructed of local materials — limestone and mud bricks made from material on the bed of the Greenough River. The local museum at Greenough houses mementos of the earliest years of pastoral settlement but reminders of Greenough's past are not restricted to the museum. A mail box, circa 1896, has given a splash of colour to the town since the reign of Queen Victoria, while the old steam engine stands in silent memorial to the heady days of the Western Australian gold boom.

Settlers' House is considered to be one of the most important historical buildings in York. Built in 1845, this two-storey brick house has a timber verandah that provides external access to the rooms of the upper floor.

St Francis Xavier Cathedral in Geraldton is a richly textured, twin-towered structure embodying Romanesque, Norman and Renaissance styles. The church was built of random freestyle stone in the Spanish colonial tradition and is considered a masterwork of the architectural genius Monsignor John Cyril Hawes.

PRECEDING PAGE:
York homesteads such as the old Mahogany Inn retain their colonial air. Indeed, York has survived largely unchanged since the 19th century.

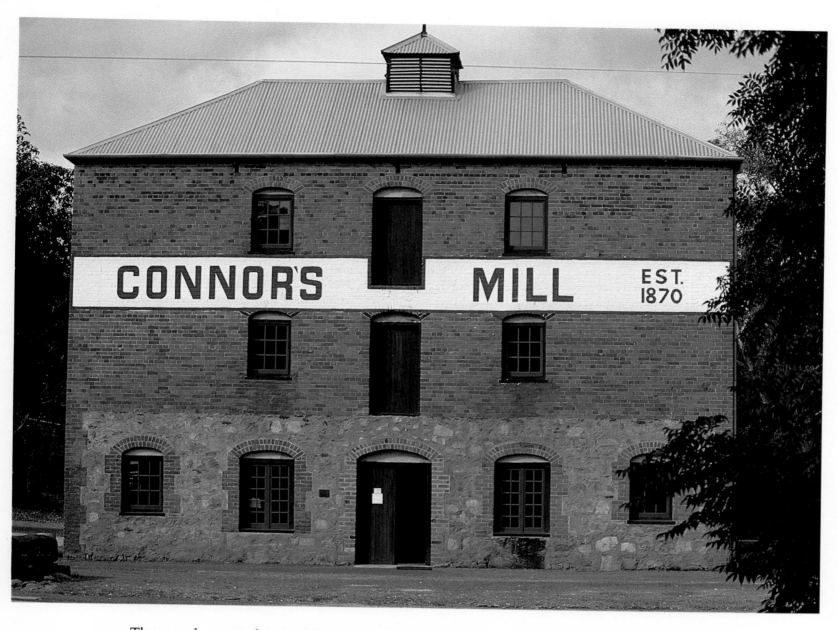

The somewhat unusual name of the Avon Valley town of Toodyay was derived from the local Aboriginal word 'duigee', meaning a place of plenty. Connor's Mill, erected in 1870, operated as a steam mill for processing the region's bountiful grain harvests for about fifty years. The old mill is now the local visitors' centre and from here one may be directed to take in a little history by reading the headstones that mark the graves of early settlers around the first church in Toodyay.

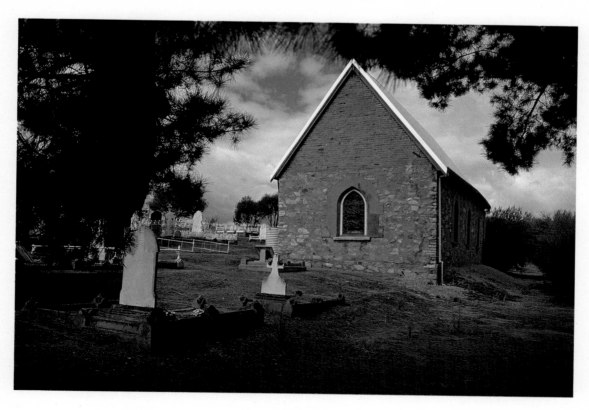

OPPOSITE PAGE: *Crayfishing is one of the most important businesses around Geraldton these days. The sources of bounty in the region have changed over the years from the tin mining and farming of the 1870s to the gold mining of the 1890s at Nannie, Cue, Day Dawn and Mt Magnet. Bounty from the Indian Ocean provides a new perspective for Geraldton in the 20th century. Crayfish are potted in the crawling season then stacked on the wharf for processing and packaging before being sent to southern markets.*

PRECEDING FOUR PAGES:
Pages 248/249: Not far from Greenough is the town of Geraldton, home of the modern Western Australian cray-fishing industry. Throughout the Geraldton-Greenough area are early crayfishermen's cottages, now abandoned. Pages 250/251: The long pier at Geraldton was built for the mining industry further upriver but became useful for transporting sheep to the pastoral country around Green-ough. Today, the uses have once again changed and now the pier is used not only for pleasure craft but also for boats of the thriving fishing industry.

Crawling lobsters brought into port are prepared and cooked for the West's restaurants and fish shops. Many of the women working in the industry were born in Europe.

*First place amongst industries in the Geraldton area is still mining.
The town is a growing industrial port serving a number of important
inland mining sites such as Mt Morgan. Huge fuel stocks are held
at Geraldton for heavy mining and farming equipment. Although
mining is the 'new' growth industry, farming is still carried out
on a large scale. The wheat silos at Geraldton are a stark contrast
to the old ways of farming but are extremely efficient in their grain
storage and loading facilities; ships berth alongside to take on
the harvest for local and overseas markets. Wheat tankers, modern
silos and fuel stores are a far cry from the first stone houses,
the steam trains and the hopes and fears of a drought-stricken
English farming community.*

Tropical Cocktail

WANDERINGS IN NORTHERN QUEENSLAND

Some places in Australia immediately capture the imagination. Obiri Rock in Kakadu National Park, the Great Barrier Reef and the Cardwell Shire are such places. Their distinctive quality demands they be experienced and renders them unique, if only because of the profound sense of exhilaration that they impart. The Cardwell Shire, south of Innisfail in Queensland, is in a deeply shaded rainforest region bordered on the coast by a glittering necklace of islands including Dunk, Goold and Hinchinbrook. Here one encounters a race of people who have adapted themselves perfectly to the tropical life of northern Queensland.

The region was first traversed by Edmund Kennedy who landed in the bay of islands south of Tam O'Shanter Point, opposite Dunk Island, in May, 1845. On a later expedition in 1848, Kennedy and eight of his party of twelve were killed by Aboriginals just south of Cape York. Further expeditions opened up the land for farming but it was not until the 1870s that sugar became the principal crop.

OPPOSITE PAGE: *Still clothed in deeply shaded rainforest, the country inland from remote Mission Beach is ideal for beachcombers and alternative settlers. During the last hundred years or so, many people have looked towards northern Queensland as a place to establish an uncluttered lifestyle free from the pressures of urban living.* (Photo — Mark Hanlon)

Mark Hanlon

❛ *Sugar growing, which of all forms of agriculture seems to suit Queensland best, might*
be in a very flourishing condition if it were not for the Queensland government. The question at issue
is this. Sugar can only be made to pay by means of coloured labour. The work in the cane fields
is not particularly destructive to European constitutions, nor particularly hard. The only thing is that
it requires many hands, and that at the high rate of wages universal in the Australian
colonies to pay the requisite number of white labourers would be working at a dead loss. Accordingly
it has long been the custom to import coloured labourers, commonly called Kanakas, from the
South Sea Islands. This 'labour traffic' as it is called is I am afraid too often but a modified slave
trade. It is difficult to persuade many colonials that there is anything particularly
wrong in killing a nigger. ❜

(Tyrwhitt, W. S. S., The New Chum in the Queensland Bush, J. Vincent, London and Oxford, 1887, pages 44-45)

Mark Hanlon

Among the steep hills around the South Johnstone River, inland from Mission Beach, old and new Australians have built up a thriving agricultural community that is responsible for the production of sugar cane. The Italians particularly have enjoyed great success as cane farmers. The first wave of Italian migration occurred in the 1890s when a number of peasant families from Piedmont and Lombardy were brought to Queensland by Signor Fraire of Townsville. They soon had enough saved between them to purchase properties around Tully and Innisfail and, today, nearly ninety per cent of the cane workers are of Mediterranean extraction.

N ORTHERN Queensland's sugar economy was aided by the 'blackbirders' who sailed off to remote islands such as the Solomons in search of unsuspecting labourers for the plantations on the mainland. Offering a few worthless trinkets they 'bought' young men for a fixed term of indentured labour: islanders worked in the manner of slaves during their term and few returned to their homeland.

Although the Kanaka trade, as it became known, has long since ceased to exist, many of the islanders' descendants still live around places like Tully and Innisfail; on the boundaries of some plantations the barrack-like quarters that were home to their grandparents or great grandparents still exist. During the Kanaka years, important landowners in the region turned their attention to sugar cane as a source of easy profit. The legendary 'Cattle King', James Tyson, selected blocks for stocking with beef cattle in the 1880s. He also planted sugar but abandoned the venture when the law prohibiting the Kanaka trade was passed.

After WWI, a new breed of farming people arrived to live in the region. Veteran soldiers took up settlement blocks around Tully, often founding new townships named after foreign places where they had seen action such as El Arish, Jaffa, Quatia and Maadi. More commonplace in name but not in style is the attractive township of South Johnstone. Located on the river of the same name, South Johnstone lives on in a time warp of its own for little has changed on the one and only main street since the early days of the sugar industry. A narrow-gauge cane rail stretches the length of the street so that drinkers enjoying a cold beer in the Criterion Hotel can watch the cane train rumbling past the doorway en route to the sugar mill at the far end of the town.

PRECEDING FOUR PAGES:

Pages 258/259: Some people find their freedom at sea. Large schooners ply the tropical waters with holiday-makers intent on recapturing some of the romance of sailing the South Seas. Sailing boats such as the trading schooners were the first to bring back Kanaka labour, from islands to Australia's north-east, for working the cane fields last century.

Pages 260/261: Over-ripe sunsets around Port Douglas, north of Cairns, are a regular feature of northern Queensland waters.

' *A percentage of the successful farmers in the Innisfail District are Italians, whose success provides an object lesson to Australians who are apt to forget that only those who venture deserve to win. Arriving in the sugar country with perhaps less than £5 in hand, newcomers from the North of Italy get to work in the cane-cutting gangs. The rates of pay for that class of work are high, and in two or three seasons the thrifty Italians save enough to pay the first deposit on a farm. In some cases they combine to secure a farm, work in the fields themselves with other Italians as their employees, who engage on the understanding that they will be paid as soon as the employers receive their money for the raw product. In a few years the full price of the farm has been paid, and the Italian owner or owners then improve the dwellings, and engage in more general spending. Determined young Australians preferably are encouraged similarly to become North Queensland sugar farmers, and prosperity and honour will be the reward of those who venture. In these days of railway communication they have facilities unknown to the earlier sugar-farmers or to that later generation of farmers who did not begin operations till the indentured island labourers had been deported. The success of the A. I. F. men south of Innisfail is guarantee for the safety of their selections or their first and subsequent deposits, should they buy land on terms of time payment.* '*

(Queensland Government Tourist Bureau, North Queensland — Australia's Richest Territory, Brisbane, 1928, page 7)

PRECEDING PAGE:
The verdant region around Tully is regarded as one of the wettest parts of Australia. The average annual rainfall of 4320 mm is partly the result of the height of the hinterland mountains. They cause the uplift of rain-bearing monsoon clouds which gather huge quantities of water.

Cane growing and transporting may be mechanised these days but back-breaking labour is still necessary for the maintenance of the industry. When the cane is first planted, weeding ensures that the Guinea grass does not choke the young cane. Later, weeding is not required since the cane blocks cut out all light necessary for the growth of weeds. Then comes the harvest. Cane cutters work approximately six months of the year during the season and after that move on to other work. In the early days, when there was little other work to be found, many of the cane cutters used to go down to the beach where they would spend the rest of the year as beachcombers. Today, railway maintenance is an important feature of the off-season. The entire sugar network is criss-crossed with a network of narrow-gauge lines linking outlying fields to the sugar mills. Repairs are carried out regularly on the lines near South Johnstone. (Photos — Mark Hanlon)

Mark Hanlon

Old cane cutters reminisce at the Criterion's bar, sometimes recalling the great cane strike of 1935 when they downed knives, refusing to cut green cane. The pub itself is a storehouse of memories and local community life. A profusion of stuffed swordfish and buffalo horns adorn the walls and St Rita's Catholic School Goose Club details a variety of tasty fare to be won for the price of a raffle ticket. First prize is a tray of vegies, a roast, a bottle of wine and a six-pack of beer. Ninth prize is a packet of biscuits. On the other side of the street and half-concealed by potted flowering plants is Coral's Cafe, just down the road from the local cinema. Now in ruins, this theatre is but a shade of its former glory with only a disordered array of stained canvas chairs and a billboard crowded with flaking, faded film posters to remind one of the days when Saturday night flicks were the social event of the week. Most persistent and pervasive of all the sensations encountered in the township is the sweet, sugary aroma that drifts back up the road from the mill.

Further down the river is another cane town. Innisfail was once a major river port for southbound boats taking on bananas but that was before the railways and highways. Sitting by the river it is not difficult to imagine cargo boats on their voyage downriver to the ocean, even though most of the vessels these days are either fishing boats or pleasure craft. All around South Johnstone and Innisfail, old plantation homesteads on stilts rise above the tall cane like sentinels. In contrast are houses reflecting distinctly Italian ideas of architecture, for many Italians have lived in the region for decades. In fact, strolling along under the shop awnings in Innisfail and Tully, the gently lilting sound of someone saying *buona sera* or *arrivaderci* is commonplace.

Mark Hanlon

Although they are pulling down the local picture theatre because of lack of patronage, little else has changed. The Criterion Hotel is a focal point for the whole community; on Saturday afternoons there will always be a few in the bar listening to the races. In silent witness to the town's reason for existence is the cane track traversing the main street.

OPPOSITE PAGE: *Further down the river from South Johnstone is the town of Innisfail, famous for its surrounding cane fields. The town is also a thriving fishing village. Italians have lived in the area for decades.* (Photo — Mark Hanlon)

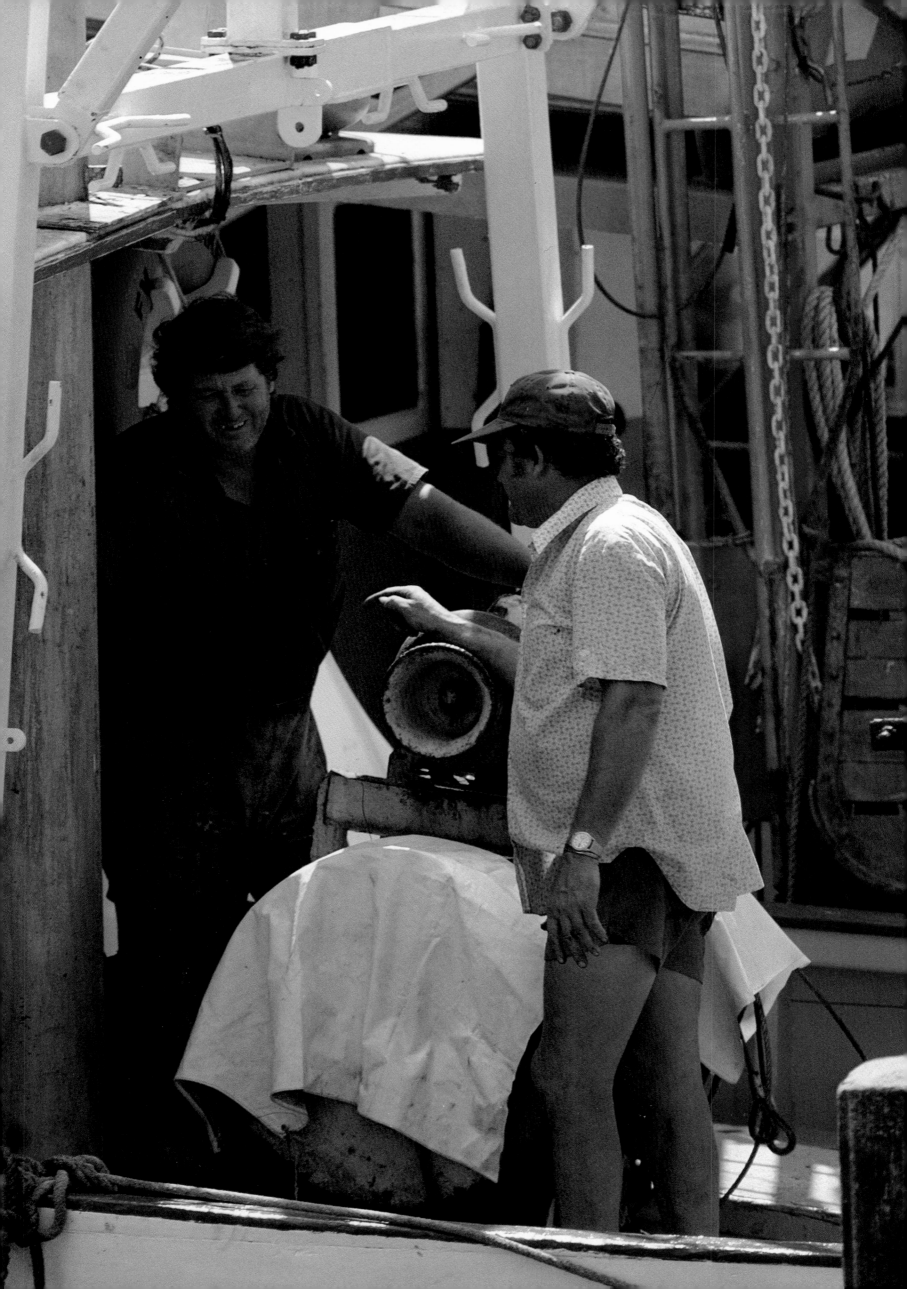

The port facilities of Innisfail have always been vital to the town's prosperity. In the old days, banana boats used to ply the section of river that is now a popular haven for tourist and fishing boats. Fishing is an important industry for people living in northern Queensland.

(Photos — Mark Hanlon)

The people who have settled in this steamy country, pungent with the heavy scents of raw sugar, tropical blooms and rotting vegetation, are a special breed who have brought with them cherished dreams in hope of fulfilment. Near Mena Creek lived Joe Paronella, a Spaniard who constructed a magnificent palace, complete with castellated towers, walkways, forest paths, theatre and his own hydro-electricity plant. It took him eighteen years from 1930 to 1948 to complete his life task, which he realised by working patiently each day with a hand-operated cement mixer that he made himself out of a forty-four gallon drum. Next to a high waterfall in northern Queensland he had recreated the glory of Castille but, after his death, Paronella Park fell into disrepair and was finally gutted by fire a few years ago. Like Don Quixote, Joe Paronella's dream of vanquishing tropical Australia was one windmill that could not be overcome.

Others come here to live in harmony with the environment. Wearing no more than sarongs and tee-shirts, younger people from southern cities have chosen to break away and start new lives in tropical hideaways amongst the lush foliage. Along the coast at places like Mission Beach, Bingil Bay and Lugger Bay they use natural forest woods to build their own Shangri-la. Some of them turn to arts and crafts, weaving baskets or painting for a living. Others simply live off the land — or the beach when the fishing is good. Of course, they are not the only ones who have chosen to live simply. The beachcomber's ways are a popular alternative along the tropical, sandy coast. A number of older men set the example, eking out an existence with the aid of their pension cheques: old cane cutters, fishermen and even remittance men from England have together made the tradition of beachcombing an (almost) respectable profession.

Looking for all the world as though it might have been a film prop in 'The African Queen', a rather ancient fishing boat is nevertheless still used on the river. A Panama hat and cream flannel trousers would not be out of place in the setting of Innisfail. Even the rowboats appear to have seen days when adventure was a constant part of northern Queensland life.

Rupert Fenby was perhaps the best known beachcomber in the locality. He built a hut in the forest and remained there until he died. They say he rarely wore clothes, preferring the natural life; to survive, he grew a few yams, bananas, coffee and tobacco plants. When he died, his body was buried not far from his hut, in the heart of his own Eden. Another beachcomber was Bill Elder who lived for many years on a headland above Bingil Bay. Bill threw away his calendar and clocks when he retreated to his hermitage and filled his life by reading philosophy out of books he would borrow from residents living along the beach. Anyone he met was immediately approached by Bill with the question, 'What day is it, if you don't mind?' The beachcomber's life is still a timeless mode of existence in a world adorned with sea shells, fresh crab and the screech of swirling sea birds offshore.

In fact, all of northern Queensland possesses a special quality not found in modern, technology-dependent cities. On the forest paths and isolated beaches and in the towns, one encounters a sense of peace and harmonious existence with the natural world.

For those with more modern tastes, the river offers plenty of space for waterskiing, sailing and all water sports. Nevertheless, I sat gazing at this part of the river wondering how surprised I might be if a banana boat were to steam into view from around the bend in the river.

One of the great beauties of northern Queensland is the richness of its tropical flora. The fruits of some are delicious to eat so it is no wonder that beachcombers regarded northern Queensland as a tropical paradise. All they needed was a piece of thatch over their heads to keep out the rain and a pair of thick soles to walk along the coral sand beaches or through the forest trees in search of fruits of the north.

PRECEDING PAGE:
North of Cairns is an idyllic tropical outpost called Port Douglas. It is a perfect tropical stepping stone when bound for the islands of the Great Barrier Reef nearby, as well as the Mossman River National Park a few kilometres to the north. From Port Douglas, too, begins the journey inland to the world famed Quinkan Reserve, home to a vast array of important Aboriginal cave art treasures.

OPPOSITE PAGE: Coconut palms flourish around Mission Beach. The coconut, a rich source of food and useful products such as fibre, drinking vessels and so on, has made it easy for beachcombers to live off the land. (Photo — Mark Hanlon)

Mark Hanlon

Some of Australia's most magnificent ferns and trees grow in abundance in the rainforest around Mission Beach. They complete a complex ecology dependent on high rainfall, steamy humidity and rich soil, offering welcome shade to a variety of ground birds such as the brush turkey. Few such stands of rainforest are left undisturbed anywhere in Australia yet even now places like Kennedy Bay to the south of Mission Beach are under threat from developers.

Dark rain clouds are a regular feature of northern Queensland and bring the rain essential for healthy growth in
the cane fields near Innisfail. Even a home field near Kuranda — on this occasion populated by a flower-bedecked horse —
reflects profuse growth in imitation of a well kept domestic garden that would be the envy of many southerners. Owing to
the hot, wet climate, plantation homesteads are normally built up on stilts to allow a flow of air underneath. The system
provides not only for cooling and drying of wet foundation timbers but also discourages the entry of unwanted house
guests such as cane toads. Some homesteads, however, have been transformed with the addition of a ground floor.
With the development of modern technology, this old style of architecture is not so essential for comfortable living.

PRECEDING PAGE:
Inland waterways offer a tranquil contrast to the riot of the jungle
ecosystem. For observing water birds or for a spot of fishing,
the waters to the west of the Great Divide are perfect.

OPPOSITE PAGE: Northern Queensland's high rate
of precipitation keeps the rivers of the Great Divide
swollen to such an extent that waterfalls abound in
the steep mountains. Once on the narrow coastal plain
between Tully and Mossman, the rivers irrigate the
fertile soil for tropical agriculture.

Private and public gardens in northern Queensland support a profusion of representative species of flora from the American, Asian and African tropical belts, quite apart from the native ferns, grasses and spectacular flowering plants such as the Australian epiphytic and terrestrial orchids.

The humid conditions of the region provide a natural hot house for exotic tropical flowers. So perfect is the environment that many of them have become naturalised along roadsides, railway lines and even in private gardens.

The Great Barrier Reef and the offshore islands located amongst the coral are an integral part of northern Queensland. Although many of the islands are now catering to large tourist complexes, it is still possible to find an uninhabited island of one's own. On small, unpopulated islands such as these, the tradition of beachcombing developed in the tradition of such men as E. J. Banfield. Banfield was probably most famous for his books, including 'Confessions of a Beachcomber', that glorified the tropical vagrant's lifestyle. He eventually died on Dunk Island where he had lived for twenty-five years.